Napoleon's Balkan Troops

Vladimir Brnardic • Illustrated by Darko Pavlovic

Series editor Martin Windrow

First published in Great Britain in 2004 by Osprey Publishing
Elms Court, Chapel Way, Botley, Oxford OX2 9LP, United Kingdom
Email: **info@ospreypublishing.com**

A CIP catalogue record for this book is available from the British Library.

ISBN 1 84176 700 X

Editor: Martin Windrow
Design: Alan Hamp
Index by Glyn Sutcliffe
Maps by Darko Pavlović,
Originated by The Electronic Page Company, Cwbran, UK
Printed in China through World Print Ltd.

04 05 06 07 08   10 9 8 7 6 5 4 3 2 1

FOR A CATALOGUE OF ALL BOOKS PUBLISHED BY
OSPREY MILITARY AND AVIATION PLEASE CONTACT:

The Marketing Manager, Osprey Direct UK, PO Box 140
Wellingborough, Northants, NN8 2FA, United Kingdom
Email: **info@ospreydirect.co.uk**

The Marketing Manager, Osprey Direct USA, c/o MBI Publishing
729 Prospect Avenue, Osceola, WI 54020, USA
Email: **info@ospreydirectusa.com**

www.ospreypublishing.com

Dedication

To my wife Teodora and daughter Helena,
and my *Grenzer* ancestors of the 4th Szluin Regiment.

Acknowledgements

Many people have helped me to prepare this book. I should like
to thank Dave Hollins and Darko Pavlović for their advice, Dave
for assistance with the text, and Darko for the plates; Madame
Vera Mihalić, my host while I was researching in Paris, and Luc
Oreskovic; Tomislav Aralica, who allowed me to draw upon both his
collection (picture credits, Aralica) and his outstanding knowledge;
Alfred Umhey, for his help with illustrations from the Sammlung
Alfred u. Roland Umhey (credits, Umhey); Dr Francesco Simoncini,
for his help with the initial research; Arsen Duplančić, of the library
of the Archaeological Museum in Split (credits, AMS); Marina
Bregovac-Pisk and Janko Jelinčić, curators of the Croatian
Historical Museum in Zagreb (credits, CHM); Ivanka Brekalo,
curator of the Samobor Museum (credits, SM); Mme Drosson, of
the International Museum of Hussars, Tarbes (credits, MIHT). Also
to the directors and staff of the Military History Museum, Vienna
(credits, MHMV); the Service Historique de l'Armée de Terre,
and Bibliothèque Nationale de France, Paris (credits, BNFP).
Notwithstanding all this valued assistance, any mistakes remain
the author's responsibility.
I should also like to thank my parents, brother, sister-in-law and
parents-in-law, but I am the most grateful to my wife Teodora for
her love, support, help and understanding.

Author's Note

This book may be read in conjunction with:
MAA 76, *Napoleon's Hussars*; MAA 88, *Napoleon's Italian and
Neapolitan Troops*; MAA 146, *Napoleon's Light Infantry*; MAA 176,
Austrian Army of the Napoleonic Wars (1): Infantry; MAA 299,
Austrian Auxiliary Troops 1792–1816; MAA 314, *Armies of the
Ottoman Empire 1775–1820*; and MAA 335, *Emigré & Foreign
Troops in British Service (1802–15)*.

Artist's Note

NAPOLEON'S BALKAN TROOPS 1797–1815

THE FRENCH EMPIRE IN THE BALKANS

THE PERIODS OF FRENCH RULE over the Ionian Islands (1797–99 and 1807–14), Dalmatia and Istria (1805–14), and finally the Illyrian Provinces (1809–14) were relatively short. However, they left a lasting mark on the history of today's Slovenia, Croatia, Albania and Greece – largely for the better, although this was not acknowledged for many years.

The first French possession in south-east Europe was the Ionian Islands, a group off the western Greek coast, often called Heptanesos (the Seven Islands, Fr. *Sept Îles*). This former Venetian possession of strategically located islands, guarding the entrance to the Adriatic Sea, was ceded to France under the Treaty of Campo Formio on 17 October 1797. In 1799 the Russians captured the islands and established an important base for their Mediterranean Fleet. In March 1800 the Septinsular Republic was created, at first under Turkish sovereignty, and then as a Russian protectorate. The Russians and French resumed their contest to control both the islands and the Adriatic during 1806; but a year later the Tsar had to return them to the French Empire under the 1807 Treaty of Tilsit. Two years later, they were amalgamated with France's mainland territories to form the Illyrian Provinces; but in late 1809 the British seized five of the seven Ionian Islands, leaving only Corfu and Paxos under French control.

The term 'Illyria' (Lat. *Illyricum*) had been used for the eastern coast of the Adriatic since Roman times, but by the 18th century it referred to the territories inhabited by Slavic peoples. The coast had been mainly under Venetian rule until 1797, when Austria added the defunct republic's possessions to its small coastal province. Following the disaster of Austerlitz in 1805, Austria ceded the former Venetian provinces of Istria, Dalmatia and the Bay of Cattaro to Napoleon. However, the Franco-Russian struggle for Adriatic domination was spreading along the Balkan coast throughout 1806–07, drawing in the Montenegrins, who sided with the Tsar. The French expanded their new territories with the seizure of the independent Republic of Ragusa (Dubrovnik) in

Marshal Auguste de Marmont, first governor-general of the Illyrian Provinces from 1806. Napoleon created his fellow artilleryman and old friend Duke of Ragusa – today, Dubrovnik. Marmont would later be reviled for his part in negotiating the 1814 truce which allowed the Allies to enter Paris, and for voting in December 1815 for Marshal Ney's execution. (Engraving by T.Johnson after J.B.P.Guérin)

THE ILLYRIAN PROVINCES
1809 - 1814

Legend:
- GAINED 1805
- OCCUPIED 1806 (REPUBLIC OF RAGUSA)
- GAINED 1809

REGIMENTAL AREAS OF
CHASSEURS D'ILLYRIE
1 - 1st Regt. (ex-Liccaner GIR No.1)
2 - 2nd Regt. (ex-Ottocaner GIR No.2)
3 - 3rd Regt. (ex-Oguliner GIR No.3)
4 - 4th Regt. (ex-Szluiner GIR No.4)
5 - 5th Regt. (ex-1st Banal GIR No.10)
6 - 6th Regt. (ex-2nd Banal GIR No.11)
Glina - REGIMENTAL HEADQUARTERS

Dalmatia and the Illyrian Provinces, 1809–14, with earlier acquisitions since 1805. In that year the French took the territories which had originally been under Venetian rule until 1797, when they had briefly passed to Austria under the peace treaty ending the War of the First Coalition.

1806. These territories were initially incorporated into the Kingdom of Italy, a satellite kingdom under Napoleon's personal rule as king since 1804.

Another defeat in 1809 cost Austria more territory, including her small coastline: the rest of Istria, Trieste, parts of Carinthia and Carniola, and Croatia south of the Sava River, including the Croat and Banal districts of the region designated as the Austrian Military Border (*Militärgrenze*). Napoleon's intention was to cut the Austrian Empire off from the sea, and to seal off the last southern access for Great Britain to European markets. At the same time, he wanted to secure French control of the Alpine passes between Central Europe and the Adriatic, in order to open land routes for French trade with the Middle East to replace the maritime routes now blocked by the Royal Navy. His 1809 gains were joined to Dalmatia and Istria on 25 December 1809, to form the Illyrian Provinces (*Les Provinces Illyriennes* – invoking the ancient name) as a direct dependency of the French Empire.

Carabiniers of the Royal Dalmatian Legion parading before Napoleon in Venice on 29 November 1807. The green uniform has red facings and distinctions, and is worn over a white waistcoat, with black half-gaiters, and French equipment including the *sabre-briquet*. The shako pompon is apparently halved red over green. (Zanoni, courtesy Umhey)

The combined provinces covered an area of about 21,500 square miles with a population of around 1,500,000. They were divided into six civil districts: Carniola; Carinthia with Villach and Linz; Istria with Trieste and Gorizia; Civil Croatia, Dalmatia with the Bay of Cattaro; the territory of the former Republic of Ragusa; and Military Croatia (*La Croatie militaire*). The administration of the provinces and the command of the Illyrian troops were entrusted to a governor-general, with his base at Ljubljana until 31 August 1813 and thereafter at Trieste. The first governor, Marshal Marmont, had the authority of a viceroy; but his successors Gens Bertrand (1811) and Junot (1813, replaced by Fouché the same year), only had the status of a prefect of the group of districts. The official languages were 'Illyrian' (Croatian, Serbian and Slovenian) and Italian, except in contacts with the central authorities. Marshal Marmont made strenuous efforts to improve the welfare of his subjects: new schools were opened, roads constructed and newspapers published. He sent two hundred sons of officers and NCOs from Military Croatia and of other prominent citizens of the provinces to French military schools.

The area's strategic position exposed it to constant threats. Britain's Royal Navy controlled the Adriatic and threatened the coast from their bases on the captured Ionian Islands and, later, from the island of Vis (Lissa), which they captured in 1812. The Turks raided Military Croatia frequently, and the Montenegrins mounted regular incursions into the Bay of Cattaro and Dubrovnik. Keen to recover their lost territories, the Austrians secretly encouraged former Grenzers (frontier troops) to desert or mutiny. After Austria had joined the Allies in August 1813, its troops invaded the provinces and retook them by January 1814; at the same time the Montenegrins, helped by the Royal Navy, took the Bay of Cattaro, but were expelled by the Austrians by June 1814. The French abandoned their last two Ionian Islands in 1814.

As in other countries occupied by the French, significant numbers of soldiers were raised, both to garrison the territory and to fight in Napoleon's campaigns. Eleven battalions totalling nearly 8,000 soldiers from the Illyrian Provinces took part in the 1812 invasion of Russia.

DALMATIA & ISTRIA

Dalmatians had a reputation as good soldiers and sailors, so Napoleon followed the previous Venetian traditions in employing them. The French raised one battalion from Istria, together with two battalions and one Legion from Dalmatia, all of which were part of the Royal Italian Army (even after the Illyrian Provinces were established in 1809). These Dalmatian troops were later merged into one regiment, while sailors were also recruited from both territories for the Royal Italian Navy.

1st & 2nd Dalmatian Battalions

Following the 1805 Treaty of Pressburg, the remnants of Austria's three Dalmatian battalions were transferred to the army of the Kingdom of Italy as the 1st and 2nd Dalmatian Battalions (*Battaglione Dalmata*) on 17 February 1806. They were under the command of a *chef de bataillon* with an adjutant-major and a quartermaster. Formed from the first two Austrian units, 1st Battalion had 27 officers, 968 NCOs and men in one grenadier and seven fusilier companies, each commanded by a captain, a lieutenant and a second-lieutenant. It was stationed first at Mantua and then at Civitavecchia in northern Italy. The 2nd Battalion (formed from the third Austrian unit) was based in Venice and attached to the Navy.

Both battalions adopted the six-company establishment of the French light infantry by an order of 18 June 1806, with a staff expanded by the addition of an adjutant NCO, a surgeon, a corporal-drummer, an armourer, a tailor and a shoemaker. A month later the 1st Battalion, 882 strong, was reorganized: each of the new six companies (four of Chasseurs and one each of Voltigeurs and Carabiniers) kept the same officer establishment, and had a sergeant major and a quartermaster corporal, four sergeants, eight corporals, two drummers (buglers for the voltigeurs), two sappers and 100 soldiers. Under the 1807 Réglement, the battalion staff was expanded to 11 by the addition of a chaplain and a wagon-master. Each company was also allowed to have two *enfants de troupe*, giving a total battalion establishment of 24 officers, 714 NCOs and men plus 12 *enfants de troupe*. In reality, the 1st Battalion numbered about 550 and 2nd Battalion 640 in 1808.

Royal Dalmatian Legion
Napoleon wanted additional troops to protect the area, so a decree of 31 May 1806 established the Royal Dalmatian Legion *(Legione Reale Dalmata)*, comprising four battalions. The Legion would be commanded by a colonel and a lieutenant-colonel with a staff of four *chefs de bataillon* each with his adjutant and an adjutant NCO, two quartermasters, a drum-major, four craftsmen and a wagon-master, on the same basis as the other Italian Army light units. Each battalion would consist of six companies with the same company establishment as the Dalmatian Battalions. Half of the officers and NCOs would be taken from the Italian or even the French Army, the others coming from Dalmatia. Two battalions were to be assembled in Zadar and two in Split. By another order from the Viceroy of Italy, Gen Eugène de Beauharnais, dated 30 June 1806, the Legion's strength was set at 2,700, later raised to 2,950 officers, NCOs and men. Recruits aged between 18 and 30 were conscripted for six years in peacetime, extended for the duration of hostilities in wartime. This conscription provoked widespread resistance, aided by the Russian Navy, but the rebellion was suppressed. Eased by a reduction in the service period to four years, recruiting restarted over the following year, but by the end of 1807 only two battalions had been raised.

Royal Dalmatian Regiment
Given the stubborn resistance to further recruitment, these two battalions of the Legion were merged with the two Dalmatian Battalions into the Royal Dalmatian Regiment *(Reggimento*

This illustration of a carabinier of the Royal Dalmatian Regiment is from regulations published in Milan in 1809. Note the red epaulettes and shako cord, red-over-green pompon, and white sword knot with red tassel. The inscription 'RRD' and the crown of Lombardy on the diamond-shaped yellow metal shako plate are shown as black. (Umhey)

Reale Dalmata). Its now four battalions were numbered by their previous seniority, but were spread out across the region: the 1st Bn was stationed in Italy, the 2nd with the Navy in Venice, and the last two garrisoned the ports of Zadar, Dubrovnik and Cattaro (Kotor) in Dalmatia.

The men of the first two battalions were experienced in mountain warfare and were initially deployed against the 1809 pro-Austrian rebellion in the Tyrol. Both then joined Viceroy Eugène's army, and the 1st Bn fought well in Gen Severoli's division at the battle of Raab on 1 June. Both units marched to Pressburg (Bratislava) before returning to the Tyrol in late 1809. During this war the 3rd Bn was stationed in Venice and supplied additional crews for Italian Navy ships, while the 4th garrisoned Lošinj (Lussino), Zadar and Dubrovnik. The carabinier detachment at Lošinj was captured by Anglo-Austrian forces after two days of fighting; four companies of chasseurs took part in the defence of Zadar against an Austrian siege. For bravery during the 1809 campaign, 13 officers and NCOs of the regiment were awarded crosses of the Legion of Honour. By the end of the year all four battalions were in Venice, from where they were sent to Treviso; during 1810–11 they were stationed in northern Italy, reinforced with recruits from Dalmatia. From 1 September 1809 the regiment had been augmented by an artillery company comprising a lieutenant and a second lieutenant, three sergeants, three corporals and 62 soldiers.

In 1812, the first three battalions and the artillery company joined the Grande Armée in Russia as part of the 15th Division (Pino) of Viceroy Eugène's IV Corps. The regiment, whose voltigeurs were noted as skilled sharpshooters, missed the battle of Borodino but entered Moscow, before fighting at Maloyaroslavec on the retreat, where it won 15 decorations. Reduced to just a single battalion by the time they reached the River Niemen, the survivors marched back to Italy, where the regiment was re-formed in Venice. When Austria declared war in August 1813, all four battalions of the regiment appear to have been stationed in Dalmatia, but within a year it had been taken into Austrian service, and was transferred to the Navy in December 1814.

Dalmatian uniforms

The **1st and 2nd Dalmatian Battalions** retained their Austrian-style uniforms but added epaulettes, rank and service stripes in the French style. The uniform consisted of a green single-breasted tunic buttoned down to the waist, with a red collar, pointed cuffs and short turn-backs, and grey Hungarian-style trousers with black or grey gaiters. Their black leather helmet was replaced by a black *corsehut* – a high-crowned round hat with a broad brim, its left side of exaggerated size and turned up

Forthoffer's rather strange reconstruction of Istrian Chasseurs, 1807–09. The chasseur (right) wears a grey jacket in the Austrian style instead of green, with sky-blue facings, over a green waistcoat. His leather accoutrements are black. The grey trousers have light blue edging to the front flap, and the black *corsehut* a light blue pompon. The carabinier (left) from 1808 wears an odd new shako with a green pompon striped and tufted red, and red epaulettes with green crescents. His jacket is otherwise like that of the chasseur, but his waistcoat is red. His green trousers have sky-blue side stripes and thigh knots; the white gaiters are trimmed sky-blue with red tassels. (Umhey)

beside the crown; the carabiniers were an exception, having a fur bonnet, red epaulettes and sword knot. The buttons were plain tin. By another order of 1 September 1806, the 2nd Bn uniform was to be essentially the same as that of the 1st (then at Bergamo), only differing by the stamped 'Secondo Battaglione Dalmata' on the buttons, and sky-blue trousers.

The July 1807 Réglement included detailed descriptions of new uniforms for the entire Royal Italian Army. However, the Dalmatians' uniforms were only altered by the change to sky-blue trousers and by new distinctions on the waistcoat, greatcoat and forage cap. The 1st Bn had a green collar and red cuffs on their red waistcoat, and the 2nd a red collar and green cuffs; the 1st Bn greatcoat was iron-grey with a sky blue collar, that of the 2nd was green with a red collar. The forage caps were iron-grey piped with green, with a red and a sky-blue tassel respectively. The chasseurs used a white sword knot and green pompon; the carabiniers wore the usual red epaulettes, pompon and sword knot; and the voltigeurs wore green epaulettes and sword knot with a yellow pompon. Otherwise, their Austrian equipment was soon replaced with French designs.

The **Royal Dalmatian Legion** wore a very similar style of uniform, differentiated only by a white waistcoat with a red collar and cuffs, together with green trousers, although the voltigeurs also had a yellow collar on the *habit*. The chasseurs initially wore soft leather *Opanke* shoes. In 1808 the entire Italian Army adopted the French-style shako, and the Dalmatian units used light infantry pompons and cords: red for carabiniers, white cords and a green-over-white pompon for chasseurs, yellow cords and pompon for voltigeurs. A diamond-shaped yellow metal shako plate bore the letters 'LRD' (Legione Reale Dalmata) under the Iron Crown of Lombardy, with an Italian white-red-green cockade. The **Royal Dalmatian Regiment** retained the Legion's uniform, except for a shako plate displaying the new initials 'RRD' (Reggimento Reale Dalmata). Their artillerymen had French-style, and train soldiers Austrian-style, green tunics piped with red on the green collar, cuffs and front edge. A green waistcoat was worn by both, with red shako cords, pompon and sword knot for artillerymen, but green for the train. In 1812 the regulation sword knot was changed to white, red for carabiniers and artillerymen, and green for voltigeurs. The chasseur pompon was also changed to white and green for voltigeurs. The men were armed with both a musket and an infantry sabre. The company of voltigeurs and some NCOs were armed with carbines, although drummers only carried sabres. The sappers carried carbines, sabres and axes.

Under the 1807 regulations, each Dalmatian battalion had one standard and two *fanions*. The

'A Morlak from the Knin area', dressed in a red cap decorated with yellow; a loose white shirt, decorated red waistcoat, green jacket trimmed with brown fur, blue breeches, multicoloured gaiters and *Opanke* shoes. Thrust under his broad brown leather belt are a pistol and long *yataghan*. Note the typically long barrel of the decorated flintlock gun. (CHM)

Royal Dalmatian Regiment received an Italian 1808 pattern standard with an Eagle; the flag was white in the central lozenge, edged by alternate green and red corners. The motto on the reverse was in Italian, probably: *'Napoleone Imperatore de' Francesi Re d'Italia allo Reggimento Reale Dalmato'.* On the obverse was the Italian eagle in gold under the imperial crown; on its breast was a red shield with the Iron Crown of Lombardy.

Royal Istrian Battalion

This *Battaglione d'Istria*, raised for coastal garrison duty, was established on 31 May 1806 with the same organization as the Dalmatian units. The battalion, which had a nominal strength of 723 officers, NCOs and men, was commanded by a *chef de bataillon* with a staff comprising an adjutant-major, an adjutant NCO, a quartermaster, a corporal-drummer and three craftsmen. The plan was to conscript 670 recruits in Istria on the same basis as in Dalmatia, but the recruiting authorities faced the same kind of response, and four months later the battalion had just 540 officers and men. Stationed at Kopar, the battalion never reached full strength (the highest figure achieved was 688 at the end of May 1807), and its reliability was so suspect that it was ordered disbanded in spring 1809, with the remnants being sent to the 1st and 2nd Italian Light Infantry Regiments. However, war with Austria produced a stay of execution, and the battalion saw action in the Tyrol. After the war ended the disbandment order was implemented in early 1810, and the men were sent to the recently formed 3rd Italian Light Infantry Regiment.

Article 12 of the 30 June 1806 decree specified the **uniform**: a short, single-breasted green *habit-veste* with seven buttons; sky-blue collar, pointed cuffs, turn-backs and piping; white waistcoat; steel-grey Hungarian trousers with sky-blue knots, black ankle boots and gaiters; black *corsehut* with a green pompon for chasseurs, red for carabiniers and yellow for voltigeurs; and a steel-grey forage cap piped sky-blue. A month later the buttons were ordered to be stamped with a hunting horn surrounded by 'Battaglione d'Istria'. The 1807 regulation confirmed the style, with the addition of a steel-grey greatcoat with a sky-blue collar. The sword knot was red for the carabiniers, green for voltigeurs and white for chasseurs; carabiniers and voltigeurs had red and green epaulettes. Each soldier was provided with two shirts, a neck-stock, two pairs of trousers, a waterbottle, leather knapsack, canvas haversack and black cartridge box. A spare pair of grey gaiters was additional to the ordinary black pair. Their armament was as for the Dalmatian battalions.

In early 1808 the headgear changed from the *corsehut* to the French-pattern peaked black

'An inhabitant of the Imotski area'; both this illustration and the Morlak depict the local costumes worn by the Pandours before French kit was introduced. His red cap is wrapped with a white turban decorated with fine red lines. His red waistcoat is partly decorated with white checkering. The green jacket has at least 16 visible buttonholes grouped in fours; scarlet turn-backs at the outside of the cuffs; and pink or purple piping at the front edge and shoulder seams. The wide white trousers are secured below the knee with tasselled red ties. He carries two pistols and a *yataghan* between different layers of his wide leather waist belt, covered with red fabric or worn under a red sash; and has a decorated brown bag slung on his hip. Note that he holds his long pipe and a tobacco bag. (CHM)

shako. The front bore an Italian tricolour cockade above a yellow-metal diamond plate, bearing 'BRI' for Battaglione Reale d'Istria under the Iron Crown of Lombardy. Like Italian light infantry regiments, the cords and pompons were red for carabiniers and green for voltigeurs; the chasseurs wore white cords with green-over-white pompons. The Istrian Battalion should have had one standard and two *fanions*.

Pandours

Pandours – a widely used name for Balkan irregulars – originated in troops raised in 16th century Dalmatia under Venetian rule, who in 1748 were organized into a police unit to guard the border with Turkish Herzegovina. The French retained this force and its organization when Dalmatia was acquired in 1805. The Pandours were initially deployed in suppressing pro-Russian rebellions and engaging the Tsar's troops in 1806, before serving as the escort to Marshal Marmont's baggage during the 1809 war, and later joining the forces of the Illyrian Provinces.

To improve their capabilities, the corps was formally organized as the **Pandours of Dubrovnik** (*Pandours de Raguse*), or **Dalmatian Pandours** (*Pandours de Dalmatie*) by a decree of 17 March 1810. Later they were also known as the **Regiment or Corps of Dalmatian Pandours**. The Pandours were recruited exclusively from amongst men in the age bracket 20–30 who lived inland, since those on the coast and islands were drafted for the navy, Royal Dalmatian Regiment or National Guard. The Pandours were stationed both in the main towns – including Zadar, Benkovac, Sinj, Vrgorac and Imotski – and in small rural garrisons. Their main tasks were guarding the north-east border against the Turks and assorted brigands; escorting couriers and caravans coming from Bosnia; and normal police duties in their districts. Exempt from peasant labour obligations, the Pandours were encouraged to perform drill and shooting practice every Sunday after Mass.

The whole corps was under the direction of a colonel stationed at Zadar, with three *chefs de bataillon*, five adjutant-majors (two captains and three lieutenants), nine captains, a paymaster, nine lieutenants and nine second-lieutenants, with 27 *harambassas* (sergeant majors) and 54 sergeants. It was made up of nine companies, each led by a captain, a lieutenant, a second-lieutenant, three *harambassas* and six sergeants; however, the companies' strength in rank-and-file varied between 36 and 48 Pandours (including two drummers), depending on the size of the administrative district to which it was assigned. In January 1811 the total strength stood at 37 officers and 475 NCOs and men. Each company was also assigned about 200 auxiliary Pandours from the local district population, who were organized as an emergency reserve.

Although they suffered high rates of desertion, these Pandours were among the few troops who offered serious resistance to the Austrian invasion in 1813. After two months of stubborn defence, their garrison in Metković (Norina) Castle on the Neretva River broke out and escaped to Herzegovina. The corps was formally disbanded after the Austrians regained control of the provinces.

The 17 March 1810 decree prescribed a **uniform** consisting of a red turban, red waistcoat, red dolman with silver lacing and trimmed with lambswool, blue trousers, Opanke sandals, white greatcoat or cloak for the men and red for NCOs. Officers used French light cavalry rank istinctions and wore hussar-style boots, although when off duty they ere allowed to wear blue French-style jackets with red facings, red reeches and silver epaulettes. Fieffé adds that regulation dress was later hanged to a blue dolman and red cloak with a French shako. Pandour eaponry was a collection of various Balkan muskets, pistols and large *ataghan* knives. Obtained locally, the muskets were either of Dalmatian pe or of regional styles such as the *šarajlija*, *čibuklija*, *rašak* or *paragun*; he same was true for the smaller weapons (see page 34).

Further south, after securing the Bay of Cattaro, the French set up a imilar unit on 1 June 1810 as the **Pandours of Cattaro,** to guard against Iontenegrin raids. This battalion was supposed to be divided into six ompanies of 50 men each, but the total never exceeded 200. On 8 November 1811 it was expanded to eight companies and its name hanged to the **Albanian Battalion** (*Bataillon Albanais*), and later to the **lbanian Pandours** (*Pandours d'Albanais*) or **Corps of Albanian Pandours** (*Corps de Pandouren de l'Albanie*). They were mostly engaged gainst irregular incursions from neighbouring Montenegro, and in the lefence of Dalmatia against Austrian invasion in 1813. The unit suffered igh levels of desertion, and by the end of 1813 it had evaporated.

The **uniform** was very similar to that of the Dalmatian Pandours, but he weapons were of characteristic local origin: the Balkan muskets were f long, thin *tančica* type, *šarajlija* from Cattaro, *arnautka*, *roga*, *rašak* or paragun; the pistols (*ledenice*, *zlatke* and *šilje*) and yataghans were usually ichly decorated with silver, brass or even gold (see pages 38 & 46). Officers and NCOs were permitted to carry either Turkish sabres or lbanian swords, tucked in the waist belt on the left side.

The long Dalmatian/Illyrian coastline required a naval force. The nitial plan was to use the ships abandoned by the Russians in 1807 (ship f the line *Sedd-el-Bahr*, taken from the Turks early in 1807; frigate Lyogkiy; corvette *Diomed*); but all these vessels were unseaworthy. Accordingly, in 1810 the **llyrian Flotilla** (*Flottille l'Illyrie*) was formed from essels previously in the lefunct Austrian Navy: wo galleys, two brigs, ten gunboats, and ten to 20 mall barques. The flotilla vas divided into three groups for coastal defence, harbour defence, and con- oying merchant shipping o protect it from British orivateers.

The crews continued o wear the dark blue Austrian naval **uniform,** since its style was similar to he French: a black round hat; a single-breasted jacket (*Paletot*) with a standing collar which bore light blue

Self-portrait of Second-lieutenant Antonio Barač of the Corps of Dalmatian Pandours, at Ljubljana on 31 May 1810, with an NCO. The officer wears the regulation Pandour uniform, which was similar to the French Chasseurs à cheval pattern, in dark blue faced and piped with scarlet, with white 'metal', and red breeches with thigh knots – note the over-knee riding boots. His sabre hangs in a steel scabbard from a red waist belt and has a silver lace knot. The shabraque is dark blue with a red line, and the valise is red. The NCO's uniform is a mixture of regulation items and native dress. See Plates C1 & C2. (AMS)

patches; a white, double-breasted waistcoat; wide sailors' trousers; low buckled black shoes, and black leatherwork. The NCOs wore a tailcoat. The French officers wore their French Navy uniforms, which comprised a single-breasted tailcoat with a scarlet collar and cuffs, gold epaulettes and buttons. A few former Austrian officers, who had not transferred to the Italian Kingdom's navy, joined the flotilla and initially wore their old uniforms until they could acquire the French version: a gold-edged bicorn, a double-breasted tail-coat with a light-blue collar, round cuffs and turn-backs; light-blue breeches, and black boots. The ships' gunners seem to have continued in their Austrian uniforms: a black felt *corsehu* with the brim turned up on the left side; a single-breasted, pike-grey jacket with a red collar, round cuffs and turn-backs, yellow buttons, white breeches and black gaiters.

ILLYRIA

(Left & centre) Austrian *Grenzer* troops in the 1798 pattern white field service jackets and sky-blue Hungarian trousers; and (right) an Illyrian Chasseur, 1810, in the new dark blue uniform prescribed by Marmont, which retained the Austrian style except for the French shako. (L.Malaspine)

The core of the Illyrian troops were six former Austrian *Grenz* regiments with more than 18,000 soldiers, who had their homes in the part of the Military Border ('Military Croatia') ceded to France in 1809. The Grenzers were based upon *zadruga* or extended family homesteads, the manpower being grouped into regiments (more an administrative than a tactical designation) along the border with the Ottoman Empire. These families were drawn both from the indigenous Croat population and a mix of Christian refugees (Catholic and Orthodox) from Bosnia settled during the 16th and 17th centuries; they had held their land from the central Austrian authorities in return for military service, both on the Border and with the field armies, in which they formed the famous Grenzer battalions.

No fewer than 16,494 Croatian Grenzers who had fought in the 1809 war were assembled at Zàla-Egérszeg in Hungary to be released from their oath of allegiance to the Austrian Emperor and disarmed before returning to their French-occupied home districts. Napoleon was aware of their great military reputation in Austrian service; and although anxious about their famous loyalty to the Habsburgs, he was equally keen to employ their specialist skills, so he sent commission to investigate the unusual Border arrangements. When he received their report, Napoleon summoned a delegation of local officers to Paris in the summer of 1810. With the active support of the governor-general Marshal Marmont (who had engaged Grenzers in his 1809 campaign in Dalmatia), they persuaded the emperor to retain the traditional system to provide substantial numbers of troops for both border defence and campaign service.

Renamed the **Illyrian Chasseur Regiments** (*Régiments de chasseurs d'Illyrie*), these former Grenzer regiments were usually referred to simply as the **'Croat regiments'** (*Régiments croates*). The Austrian numbering was largely retained: 1. Licca, 2. Ottocac, 3. Ogulin, 4. Szluin, 10. (1st Banal) and 11. (2nd Banal) Regts became 1st to 6th Illyrian Regts respectively. The Border districts were placed under Gen Delzons, the commander of Military Croatia, based at Karlstadt (Karlovac). A decree of 12 February 1810 grouped the six regiments into two divisions: 1st, comprising the 3rd to 6th Regts, with headquarters at Ljubljana, and 2nd, combining the 1st and 2nd Regts with the Dalmatian Pandours Regt and having its headquarters at Zadar. As all the senior commanders had emigrated to Austria their positions were initially filled by French officers. Although some local officers were promoted during French rule, the Chasseur regimental commanding officers remained French apart from Col Sljivarić of the 1st Regt, formerly a major in the Austrian service.

The regiments retained their Austrian organization. A peacetime establishment, comprising two battalions of six companies plus a reserve

Illyrian Chasseurs officers and administrative staff, 1810 uniform. (Left to right) Staff captain in white trousers and waistcoat, with gold collar lace; *commissaire inspecteur* in the rank of brigade-general, with silver lace embroidery at collar and cuff; captain, 3rd Regt, yellow facings and lining; colonel, 6th Regt, green facings and lining – both have black hussar boots with silver trim; and engineer *chef de bataillon* in French engineer uniform. (L.Malaspine)

Regt Lylina 1811. (5ª)   Regt Ottoteats 1811. (2ª)

Sergent   Officier?

(Left) Sergeant, 5th Regt of Illyrian Chasseurs, 1811, wearing a formerly brown jacket dyed 'dark blue' (actually a dirty black), faced, lined and piped sky-blue. His shako, *Hausmontur* white trousers and the cut of the jacket reveal the uniform's Austrian origins, with only the white-red-blue cockade and silver sergeant's rank chevrons in French style. (Right) Officer, 2nd Regt of Illyrian Chasseurs, in the prescribed French uniform: dark blue faced and lined dark red, with a white waistcoat and belt and yellow 'metal' – the strap of the gold epaulette has a scarlet centre stripe. (R.Forthoffer, courtesy Umhey)

division (two companies), was expanded to a many as four battalions in wartime. The staf consisted of 17 officers: a colonel, a lieutenan colonel, two majors, an adjutant-major, an admin istrative captain and second-lieutenant, three auditors, two accountants, a regimental adjutant a regimental surgeon, two battalion surgeons and an accountant, plus 31 NCOs and soldiers: six cadets, three quartermasters, six administrative quartermasters, a drum-major, six standard bearers, eight musicians, a provost and eigh officers' servants. Each regiment should have fielded 2,507 officers, NCOs and men. The regiment's administrative staff (*Extra-Personnel* also included civilians: Catholic priests, teachers forest rangers, postmen, customs officers, a veterinarian, a midwife, and clock repairmen taking the total regimental personnel to 2,680.

Each company was under the command o four officers; a captain, a lieutenant, a second lieutenant and an ensign (the French Army di not have a rank equivalent to Fähnrich, so all these ensigns were promoted to second lieutenant). The former ranks of Feldwebel Korporal and Gefreiter were redesignated a French sergeants major, sergeants and corporal respectively; each company had a sergeant major six sergeants, eight corporals and two drummers, two pioneers, 20 sharp shooters and 160 soldiers with four servants. The famous *Doppelstutzer* (double-barrelled rifle/muskets) had been spirited away to Austria depots, so the sharpshooter detachments were soon abolished, bu the regiments retained the 50-strong artillery detachments with thei light pieces. Each company's administrative staff included a militar component of a second-lieutenant (with an administrative lieutenant fo each division of two companies), a sergeant major and eight corporal (with an administrative sergeant for each division).

Including the officers without commission and drummers withou place (supernumeraries) but excluding administrative staff, the whol force totalled 18,197 men on 1 January 1810. The initial linguisti problems were resolved by the translation of the French drill manual into Croatian in 1811. Croatian officers were also temporarily attache to French units based in the Balkans, and French NCOs were assigne to each Chasseur battalion. In 1810 a French military school was opene at Karlovac, attended by six cadets from each regiment.

In addition to field service the Illyrian Chasseurs were also deploye in small units on border duty and as temporary garrisons in the town and islands along the Adriatic coast (Rijeka, Senj, Zadar, Dubrovnik Kotor and Krk, Cres, Vis and Lastovo). In the course of these duties the were regularly engaged in repelling parties of Turkish and Montenegrir irregulars, as well as dealing with assorted bands of brigands, and alon the coast they faced British naval raids. There were two large-scal engagements with the Turks. In May 1810 Marshal Marmont led ar expedition of two French and four Croatian battalions with 800 horses and 20 guns against them. Defeated, the Turks were inactive for the next three years. In 1813, after French defeat in Russia, they attacked again towards Cetin, but although most of the Illyrian line units were absent they were checked by reserve battalions and 220 hussars from the newly formed Croatian Hussar Regiment.

In 1812, each regiment expanded its reserve division into a full 3rd Bn of less able-bodied men. Aside from a field battalion each from the 3rd and 4th Regts, these units were the only Illyrian Chasseurs remaining in the Illyrian Provinces when Austria declared war in August 1813. The Austrian army sent Grenzer units from the rest of the Military Border to re-occupy the provinces; this quickly persuaded the Chasseurs to return to their historic allegiance with almost no resistance. By early 1814 the Illyrian Chasseurs had ceased to exist.

Uniforms

Initially the Illyrian Chasseurs continued to wear their old Austrian dress – a mixture of the 1798 pattern campaign service *Feldmontur* (white jacket and Hungarian blue trousers), and the Border service *Hausmontur* (brown jackets and white trousers). The white single-breasted jacket had facings on a standing collar, on pointed cuffs with white 'bear's claw' (*Bärentatzen*) lace decorations, and on the turn-backs; the brown Hausmontur jacket had plain cuffs without Bärentatzen. Marmont's order of 28 December 1809 required the removal of all Austrian features – the yellow-black pompon, shako rosette and trouser decoration – and their replacement by French cockades and rank distinctions and the Imperial French eagle shako badge. Nevertheless, the uniform retained its former style: a white or dark brown jacket with skin-tight, light blue trousers and Hungarian ankle boots or black French shoes.

This is how the uniform was supposed to look according to the Austrian regulations, but since the troops had a part in it themselves the practice was somewhat different. The headgear was usually a tall, peakless cylindrical felt hat (*Klobuk*); the trousers sometimes lacked the usual black-yellow braiding, or were simply replaced with homemade

Spirited little drawings of a chasseur, drummer, chasseur in greatcoat, and sapper of Croatian Provisional Regiments, 1812–13. Note that the chasseurs are without sabres. The first chasseur wears a green coat, white waistcoat and yellow-striped green trousers. The drummer wears the same jacket with white-laced red 'swallow's nests' on his shoulders; both have yellow collar and cuff facings, the collars edged red and with an additional red patch supposedly worn by the 1st Provisional Regt, but this is not certain. The drummer has a green-tufted red pompon, white or straw-colour trousers, a white apron and drum cords, and a brass drum with sky-blue hoops. The greatcoated figure has a black waterproof shako cover with protruding blue pompon, a yellow patch on the collar of the beige coat, and an eagle badge on the cartridge box. The sapper has a fur *bonnet* with red cord and white-tipped red plume; a light grey coat with a red collar patch; white epaulettes with red crescents; a red chevron above white crossed axes on his sleeve; white crossbelts with brass decorations, and an eagle-pommel sabre. (R.Forthoffer, courtesy Umhey)

The only known pictorial source for a Croatian regiment in green uniform is this naif miniature portrait of an officer of (probably) the 3rd Provisional Regiment. His yellow plume and oddly-drawn embossed hunting horn on the white metal shako plate suggest that he is probably a captain of voltigeurs. There is a vague indication of a lace top band on the shako; the cockade is shown as white-blue-red from the outside inwards. The uniform is entirely green, with yellow facings, piping, and epaulette *brides*; the epaulette and contre-epaulette are shown as heavily worked silver lace. The dark line above the collar is not piping, but an almost hidden stock. (Umhey)

white trousers. The troops also preferred the soft leather Opanke shoes and high, multicoloured woollen socks to boots and gaiters. All leatherwork was to be black from 1809, but the previous Austrian white belts did not disappear completely; and a simple haversack was often carried in place of the regulation knapsack.

The Reserve Grenzers, who stayed in the Military Border to perform frontier service, used mostly local Balkan-style muskets, so the Illyrian Chasseurs field battalions were all issued with French or captured Austrian and Venetian weapons. Napoleon's unease about their ultimate loyalties meant that only Bosnian raids and the appeals of Marshal Marmont brought a steady stream of new weapons. Napoleon was also reluctant to spend money on uniforming 18,000 men who would usually be on border guard service and already had homemade uniforms for that role. Nevertheless, on 22 May 1810 Marmont prescribed a new uniform: a French shako, a blue single-breasted jacket with a collar, pointed cuffs, turnbacks and lapels faced in regimental colour; pewter buttons bearing the regimental number; a white waistcoat; blue breeches; short black Hungarian-style ankle boots or short black gaiters with the upper edge cut to resemble Hussar boots; and a beige greatcoat. The buttons, decorations, epaulettes and sword knots for officers were silver. The continued use of the Austrian style mean that the uniform could be introduced quickly and cheaply by dyeing old Austrian jackets; however, the result was more black than blue, especially when treating dark brown tunics. The regulations were quickly adjusted to permit black tunics and plain white trousers until blue material could be obtained, although the Hungarian blue trousers were also still in use. The results were probably better with the old white Austrian field service Feldmontur. The facing colours were as follows:

	Old Austrian uniform	New French uniform
1st Regt	Violet	Red
2nd Regt	Violet	Crimson
3rd Regt	Orange-yellow	Yellow
4th Regt	Orange-yellow	Violet (from June, *aurore*)
5th Regt	Crimson	Sky-blue
6th Regt	Crimson	Green

Buttons were yellow metal for the odd-numbered and white metal for the even-numbered regiments. Aside from the black leather cartridge box and scabbard, all leatherwork remained white.

By another decree of 17 June 1810 Marmont prescribed new uniforms for the administrative staff: a dark blue single-breasted jacket with nine buttons, dark blue or white trousers and waistcoat distinguished by different facings, piping, buttons, gaiters, epaulettes and sword knot. However, only the officers would have been able to purchase the dark blue cloth for their new uniforms, and some colonels may have provided new uniforms for standard-bearers and drummers.

The change started in the summer, but soon stopped when the Paris authorities decided on a green uniform for the Illyrian Chasseurs. Marmont strongly opposed the idea in a letter to the Minister of War on 26 October 1810:

'…By means of the Croatian officers who are in Paris, General Andreossy ordered any change of uniform to be stopped, because a new organization, new uniforms, etc., will be instituted… General Andreossy cannot even imagine that a simple question of uniform, which means nothing anywhere else, is very important here, because it is a question of imposing an extra burden on the families, who provide the soldiers' uniforms; if the uniforms were prescribed in the way that the families cannot make them themselves, i.e. that the families have to buy them, this single order would cause a revolution and the emigration of a large number of those, who would be unable to comply with this demand…'

The introduction of a new uniform was immediately suspended and was in fact never implemented in the Provinces, but also had the effect of stopping the introduction of the blue uniforms. Thus the troops sent to Germany and Italy in 1813 apparently wore variations of the brown Austrian uniforms.

Although the organizational tables list six standard-bearers, there is no evidence that the Illyrians were ever given Eagles. Just one white *fanion* of the 3rd (Ogulin) Regiment's 1st Battalion has survived, and presumably the other battalions also carried them.

Field service: the Croatian Provisional Regiments

Continuing Austrian Grenzer practice, the Illyrian Chasseurs never served on campaign as complete regiments, but operated as independent battalions. The high casualties sustained by the Grenzers over the previous 20 years initially made it difficult for each regiment to provide more than one battalion for field service, so these battalions were paired into four **Croatian Provisional Regiments** (*Régiments provisoires croates*) of two battalions each. The first to be ready was the 3rd Provisional Regiment, organized from the 1st Bns of 5th and 6th Regts of Illyrian Chasseurs (formerly 1st and 2nd Banal Regts) on 21 September 1811.

Officier Supérieur   Tambour-Major   Officier   Officier

A senior officer, drum-major, and two officers of Croatian Provisional Regiments, 1812–13. All three officers have green coats, yellow facings with red collar edging and patches, silver 'metal', and green breeches or trousers with yellow stripes. The right hand figure is probably from a carabinier company, given his dark brown fur busby with red pompon and bag, and red waistcoat. The greatcoats are carried rolled over the right shoulder; three are shown as light brown, the carabinier's as grey. The *tambour-major* has yellow-striped grey trousers; his lace is silver, including collar and cuff edging and a *contre-epaulette*. (R.Forthoffer, courtesy Umhey)

17

RIGHT **Second and Third Eagle-bearers of the 3rd Croatian Provisional Regt, 1812–13; this regiment certainly had an Eagle and the traditional three bearers.** (Left) Shako with red plume, white lace (silver?) edged red, brass chin scales. Blue-shafted halberd with tricolour pennon. Yellow-piped green jacket, yellow collar, red edge and patch, yellow cuffs; silver chevrons on red backing; brass scale epaulettes, silver crescents, red fringes; white metal buttons. Green breeches, no stripe; black gaiters cut like hussar boots, yellow trim and tassels. Brass-furnished white crossbelts; brass-furnished black single pistol holsters at waist. (Right) Steel helmet, black fur turban, red roach, brass chin scales. Blue-shafted pike, tricolour pennon. Green jacket, yellow facings; red service chevrons above silver-on-red rank chevrons; red epaulettes, silver crescents. Yellow-striped green breeches, gaiters as other figure. Brass-furnished white crossbelts; brass-furnished black double pistol holster at waist; white sabre knot, red tassel. (R.Forthoffer, courtesy Umhey)

FAR RIGHT **Drummers of Croatian Provisional Regiments, 1812–13.** (Left) Note the Imperial livery, probably used by the drummers of 3rd and 1st Regts; yellow facings, piping, stripes and 'swallow's-nests' on his green uniform; and his yellow waistcoat. The shako has a yellow-tufted dark blue pompon and white metal eagle plate. (Right) The grenadier drummer of the 5th (?) has a red-furnished shako; a sky-blue jacket with yellow facings and some kind of tricolour livery lace; a white waistcoat; green breeches; and yellow-trimmed hussar-cut gaiters with red tassels. (R.Forthoffer, courtesy Umhey)

The 1st Provisional Regiment, formed from the 1st Bns of the 1st and 2nd Illyrian Chasseurs (Licca and Ottocac) followed on 26 October. The 2nd Provisional Regiment, formed from the 2nd Bn of the 3rd and 1st Bn of the 4th Chasseur Regts (Ogulin and Szluin), was only ready some time after 25 February 1813; and the 4th, formed of the 2nd Bns of the 5th and 6th Regts, not before August 1813. Upon these mergers, the battalions adopted the French light infantry organization of a carabinier, a voltigeur and four chasseur companies.

The 1,860 men of **3rd Croatian Provisional Regt** were assembled in May 1811 at Ljubljana to garrison the city, under Etienne Joly, colonel of the 5th Illyrian Chasseurs. This 3rd Regt was sent to Dijon, but due to some desertions Napoleon ordered it to Paris, where he reviewed it in person on 8 December 1811 amidst an organized display of fraternity by the Imperial Guard, and officers were invited to dine with the marshals. The regiment received new green uniforms, arms and equipment and was allocated a company of artillery. It drilled frequently and took part in a few parades. Some soldiers and 13 officers, mostly Orthodox by faith, were sent home because of their possible sympathies with Orthodox Russia, and replaced with Frenchmen. Before leaving Paris, 3rd Provisional Regt received an Eagle personally from Napoleon on 4 February 1812. Two days later it was sent east to join the Grande Armée for its Russian campaign.

At Wirballen on 18 June it was reinforced with 100 soldiers sent from the Military Border, so that at the beginning of campaign the regiment's strength stood at 41 officers, 1,582 NCOs and men, together with 33 horses for artillery and train with 17 for officers. Brigaded with the 4th Swiss Regt under Gen Amey in the 9th Division (Merle) of Oudinot's II Corps, the 3rd Regt fought with distinction at both battles of Polotsk. Having lost two officers and 50 men in skirmishes north of the city on 27 July and 3 August, the regiment was cited in Gen Merle's report on the first battle of Polotsk on 18 August for distinguishing itself by repulsing a Russian charge; this action cost the regiment 200 casualties, but it was compensated with six crosses of the Legion of Honour.

The 3rd Regt was then brigaded under Gen Candras with the 1st and 2nd Swiss Regts, and concern for national honour quickly grew into rivalry. In the second battle of Polotsk (18–20 October) the French were on the defensive, but these regiments sought to surpass each other in a ferocious counter-attack. Facing the entire Russian I Corps under Count Wittgenstein, the charge was carried too far and all three regiments suffered heavily when the Russians sent in their reserves. Although it was rewarded with six more crosses of the Legion, the 3rd Croatian Regt had suffered its heaviest losses in a single action: 387 men killed or captured, one officer killed and nine wounded including Col Joly.

Although victorious at Polotsk the French had to continue their retreat. These three Croat and Swiss units were assigned the difficult task of forming a rearguard. The 3rd Regt was still a cohesive fighting force when it reached the Beresina, where the men participated in both the construction of bridges and skirmishing with the Russians on the far side of the river. With other units of II Corps, the regiment fought in the battle of 28 November, sustaining (including the previous skirmishing) about 400 casualties and 18 wounded officers as it sacrificed itself against the encircling Russians to allow the Grande Armée to escape.

By the time the regiment re-crossed the Niemen it was reduced to 13 officers and 296 NCOs and men, and had ceased to function as a separate unit. Once the stragglers had caught up, approximately 300 men of the 3rd Provisional Regt were gathered at Marienburg in January 1813. A detachment of three officers and 116 men stayed in the city, while others were sent to Magdeburg and three officers and 116 men were left in Erfurt. Seven officers and 64 men arrived at Ingolstadt on 8 April, where on 15 July 1813 they were joined by 1,200 men (200 from each Illyrian Chasseur regiment), to form a new 2nd Bn of the 1st Provisional Regiment. This battalion returned to Magdeburg, but the harsh winter and supply failures had already prompted 400 to desert before the rest surrendered to the Allies on 23 May 1814. These 25 officers and 593 men refused to march to Metz and opted to return to Austrian service. The 3rd Croatian Provisional Regiment thus ceased to exist, although it was never formally disbanded, since the detachment at Marienburg retained the title and then joined the garrison of Küstrin, which surrendered on 20 March 1814.

The Erfurt detachment was met by Napoleon while he was passing through the city in late April 1813. Remembering the regiment's outstanding service on the Beresina, he decorated one officer with the Legion cross and incorporated the detachment in the Young Guard 'to guard the Emperor's own field baggage'. In this capacity they served at Leipzig, where they lost 40 men, but there were still 152 men attached to Imperial Headquarters (although that figure might include a few additions) when they were released from service on 17 April 1814 at Fontainebleau.

(Left) Officer, 1st Croatian Provisional Regt, battle of Witebsk, 1812. Green coat with facings and lapel piping yellow, silver epaulette; white waistcoat, yellow-striped green breeches, silver-trimmed hussar boots. Note that the only shako decoration is a French cockade and silver top band – there is no plate. (Right) Officer, 3rd Croatian Provisional Regt, battle of Polotsk. His shako has an elaborate silver top band of interlinked rings, and a white metal eagle plate. His coat is a green *surtout* – the French officer's undress single-breasted, long-tailed coat; although usually in a single colour, this one is piped yellow, with yellow cuffs, and a yellow collar with a sky-blue patch with long upper extension. His waistcoat is green; his straight, loose trousers seem to have a silver side stripe. (R.Forthoffer, courtesy Umhey)

Grenadier and sappers of Croatian Provisional Regiments, 1812. The grenadiers probably never received the fur *bonnet*, shown here with red embellishments. The coat is beige with a red collar patch, the epaulette red with a white crescent, the service and rank chevrons red and white respectively. The sapper of the 5th (?) wears a hussar busby with red plume and yellow bag; his sky-blue coat is faced and piped yellow with red epaulette and sleeve badge, but is worn with yellow-striped green breeches, tucked into hussar-cut gaiters. The sapper from the 1st wears the grenadier *bonnet* with a red plume and white cord; his all-green uniform is faced, piped and striped yellow, with red collar patch and edging, red chevrons and epaulettes, and white sleeve badge. These images almost certainly represent the ideal rather than the reality. (R.Forthoffer, courtesy Umhey)

The **1st Croatian Provisional Regiment** was formed up and re-equipped in Trieste and Verona under Col Marko Šljivarić, former commander of 1st Illyrian Chasseurs. In Verona it was brigaded with the French 8e Léger and 84e de Ligne in the 13th Division (Delzons) of Viceroy Eugène's Italian IV Corps. At the beginning of the 1812 campaign the regiment's strength was 45 officers and 1,462 NCOs and men and 8 horses. It first saw action at Ostrovno on 26 July, when it was almost overwhelmed by a cavalry charge, but it managed to earn a favourable mention in the 10th Bulletin of the Grande Armée; one officer was killed and nine wounded, among them Col Šljivarić, and other casualties totalled 425 NCOs and soldiers. In a review on 22 August in Smolensk the regiment was singled out for praise by Napoleon, who awarded it six crosses of the Legion of Honour. At the battle of Borodino the regiment formed part of the second battle line under Gen Delzon, who was supporting the units in Borodino village; it had to form a square with other regiments to repulse Russian cavalry charges, but suffered few casualties. The 1st Croatian Provisional Regt marched on to reach Moscow, where the emperor allotted it another six crosses on 18 October.

During the subsequent retreat the regiment suffered a high toll including 13 officer casualties in the ferocious battle of Malojaroslavetz on 24 October. Additional losses were sustained at Vjazma on 3 November and Krasnoe on 17 and 19 November, and many more at the Beresina: just 22 officers and 31 NCOs and men survived to the end of the campaign. The regiment was warmly praised by Gen Delzons; even Napoleon was impressed by their mutual loyalty, when two carabiniers, Marko Kokotović and Milin Grubić from the Ottocac battalion, both being severely wounded in the legs, loaded their muskets and simultaneously killed each other to end their misery. Colonel Šljivarić was promoted to *général de brigade* and sent back to Croatia to raise more troops, while the remains of the regiment joined the garrison of Glogau fortress.

There on 19 February 1813 they were merged with a mixed detachment of about 1,000 reinforcements despatched by Gen Šljivarić from the 1st, 2nd, 5th and 6th Illyrian Chasseurs, to form a new 1st Bn of the 1st Croatian Provisional Regiment. The unit served with distinction during the first blockade of Glogau from 1 March to 31 May 1813, and during the summer it was combined with a battalion from the 2nd Provisional Regt to form a 'Brigade of Croats'. After the second blockade on 17 August turned into a siege their morale fell quickly; desertions increased and the remainder became mutinous. The commander of the garrison wanted to release them from service, but they refused to leave before receiving their due wages. After they were paid for two months, they left on 26 January 1814.

Shortly after being formed at Trieste in 1813 the **2nd Croatian Provisional Regiment**, with a strength of about 1,800 men, was sent to Germany, where it joined the 12th Division (Morand) of Gen Bertrand's

IV Corps. The regiment was led by Col Robert de Gordon, former commander of the 2nd Illyrian Chasseurs, and later by Col Josef Mamula. Initially assigned to guard supply trains against Prussian raids, the regiment then participated in Bertrand's successful assault on the Allied centre during the second day of the battle of Bautzen (21 May), earning five crosses of the Legion of Honour. The regiment lost two officers killed and nine wounded, and was reduced to less than 650 effectives. While Col Mamula and a cadre from the 2nd Bn returned to Croatia to raise more recruits, the under-strength 1st Bn, under the command of *Chef de bataillon* Vinisch, joined the 1st Bn of the 1st Provisional Regt in Glogau (see above), where both remained until their departure in January 1814.

The **4th Croatian Provisional Regiment** was formed at Montechiaro in Italy and was attached to Viceroy Eugène's army, but apparently never saw action. Considered unreliable, the regiment was sent to Corsica in November 1813 to be disarmed and converted to Pioneers. The regiment was formally disbanded at Ajaccio on 23 January 1814, and its officers and men incorporated into the 2nd Colonial Battalion; but they were repatriated in May.

Uniforms

The **3rd Croatian Provisional Regt** had arrived in Paris and paraded before the emperor '...in old Austrian uniforms, the only change being that the Austrian cockade was replaced with the French one.' An unhappy Napoleon ordered the Minister of War to design a new uniform for the Provisional regiments, and the old proposal of introducing a green uniform was revived. This consisted of a green jacket and trousers, with crimson facings in the light infantry pattern, white buttons and a waistcoat. Napoleon made a minor alteration in changing the facings to yellow, and to increase production rates he sent six Imperial Guard tailors to each battalion. Just a month later, in early January 1812, the Croats were issued with their new green uniform.

The jacket was of the old light infantry style, open from the chest downwards, with yellow facings on the collar and pointed cuffs, and yellow piping on the turn-backs, lapels and shoulder loops. The cara-biniers wore red epaulettes, the chasseurs red with yellow fringes and the voltigeurs green with yellow fringes. The breeches were decorated on the seam in yellow, and the short black gaiters had a yellow, tasselled hussar-style top edge. On field service long trousers with yellow

Officers, drummer and chasseur of 2nd Croatian Provisional Regt in Germany, 1813. They are all wearing the brown uniform with yellow facings; the officers have white 'metal' and white breeches; the officer on the left has a waterproof cover over his bicorn, and 'jockey' boots with loops and tan turn-overs. The drummer wears a beige greatcoat. The chasseur's trousers are decorated with the yellow side stripe, although his uniform is clearly Austrian except for the French cockade, green pompon and green epaulettes with red crescents. (R.Forthoffer, courtesy Umhey)

side-stripes were worn, with white gaiters in the summer. The waistcoat was white, and the greatcoat of smooth beige cloth. A white metal eagle plate on the shako was stamped with the regimental number in the loop of a hunting horn. The carabiniers' shakos were distinguished by a red upper edge band, side chevrons, pompon and plume; the voltigeurs by a yellow upper band and side-chevrons, a red pompon and red plume with a yellow tip, though plain yellow plumes and pompons were apparently also worn. The chasseurs used a flat, conical tufted pompon in company colour. The leatherwork and armament were of the French light infantry style, and French rank insignia included a gorget for the officers. The carabiniers had a red and voltigeurs a yellow sword knot. Drummers wore the recently introduced green 'Imperial Livery', although some may still have worn the light blue uniform.

Napoleon sent his ADC Gen Mouton to inspect the new uniform. When he reported on 19 January, he requested that 19 old Austrian muskets be replaced; he also proposed that the emperor should '... order the addition of the grenade and hunting horn emblem on the turn-backs of the carabiniers and chasseurs; that the turn-backs of the sappers should be decorated with axes and they should receive axes, axe cases, aprons, cartridge boxes, shoulder-belts and carbine-straps; there is also a need of strong belts for the Eagle-bearers and lace for the chevrons for the 2nd and 3rd Eagle-bearers.'

The last of the Austrian muskets were replaced with new French weapons, but when the regiment were supposed to leave Paris they still lacked much of their equipment. A dissatisfied Napoleon wrote on 31 January to the Minister-Director of War Administration, Count Cessac: 'The Croats in Paris have just one shirt, one pair of shoes and they do not have neck-stocks; your first task is not completed and they will stay in Paris until everything is completed. It is inconvenient that their uniform is not of new model. Their shakos are poor quality.'

On the last inspection by Marshal Berthier on 3 February before their departure each man received two pairs of new shoes. They still lacked leather belts and arms for the Eagle-bearers, as well as arms and cartridge boxes for the sappers. Much of this did catch up with the regiment once it was in Germany, and eventually the 3rd Croatian Provisional Regt was better equipped than many French regiments. Having received little new equipment in Austrian service, and delighted by their reception in Paris, the Croats lived up to their former reputation in French service and fought valiantly for the emperor.

The **1st Croatian Provisional Regt** was equipped at Trieste in December 1811. Before departure on 22 January 1812 each soldier had one pair of old and two pairs of new shoes, trousers and grey gaiters. Nevertheless, '... the Croat regiment of 13th Division arrived in Verona in a poor state: aside from regulation uniforms, they needed a lot of things like shoes, backpacks, muskets, train wagon and military hospital...'

Trooper of Croatian Hussar Regt, 1813, in the regulation uniform: 1810 pattern black shako with elite company red pompon, cockade, and white diamond plate; sky-blue dolman with buff facings; white and crimson barrel-sash; iron-grey pelisse trimmed black; all cord and lace trim white; iron-grey breeches with white decorative knots from the edges of the front flap. The black fleece saddle cover has buff 'wolf tooth' edging. (L.Malaspine)

Re-equipment proceeded slowly, so the regiment was the last to leave Verona and only rejoined its division at Glogau. On parade, the uniforms and weapons were discovered to be of poor quality, and 700 replacement muskets had to be requested.

The **2nd and 4th Croatian Provisional Regts** never received the new green uniforms, so they joined the Grande Armée in their old Austrian-style uniforms. Contemporary sources suggest that these were entirely brown with yellow or red facings, the only French features being the cockade, pompon and epaulettes.

Only the 3rd Croatian Provisional Regt definitely received an Eagle standard, presented by Napoleon himself and probably of the new 1812 pattern. The lettering on the obverse was probably: *'L'Empéreur Napoléon au 3eme Régiment Provisoire Croate'*, but the reverse was blank. The 1st Provisional Regt may also have received an Eagle, but the other two did not.

Illyrian Regiment

Early in 1810, Napoleon wanted to raise a regiment from the people in the non-Frontier parts of the Illyrian Provinces: Civil Croatia, Rijeka (Fiume), former Austrian Istria, the provinces of Carniola and Carinthia, plus Gorizia with Trieste. Created by a decree of 16 November 1810 and formed by the end of the year at Ljubljana, the Illyrian Regiment (*Régiment d'Illyrie*) was raised around a reserve company formed by Marshal Marmont in early 1810 from officers and soldiers of disbanded Austrian regiments previously recruited in these areas.

The Illyrian Regiment was assembled at Turin in Italy to be uniformed and equipped. It was organized as a light infantry regiment, initially with one depot and three field battalions. In 1811 it was ordered expanded to five battalions and was incorporated into the French Army, conscription being introduced the same year. However, desertions and the avoidance of conscription made for constant difficulties in filling its ranks. The commander of the regiment was a veteran officer, Col Nicolas Schmitz, and a third of the officers were French, the remainder being Belgians and former Austrian officers from the depot in Passau. Still short of officers, the unit was permitted by an Imperial order to enlist Illyrian former officers of the Austrian Army. The supply of clothing was no better: '...the jackets were too small and had not been properly lined, holes for buttons were just cut out and not bound, shirts were too short, the shoes did not fit, the backpacks were of bad quality and less than half the required number of shakos had been delivered.'

The four field battalions of the Illyrian Regt were ready for active service in January 1812, and were brigaded with the 2nd Portuguese Regt in 10th Division (Razout) of Marshal Ney's III Corps. At the beginning of the Russian campaign it stood at a total of 65 officers and 2,505 NCOs and privates (accompanied by a particularly large fife band, who would also go into battle). In the first phase of the campaign the regiment only marched to Kovno and Minsk to form their garrisons. Considerable desertion led to Napoleon allowing the incorporation of 500 Lithuanian recruits on 24 August. On 19 August part of the regiment joined Ney's corps in the bloody battle of Valutina-Gora (Lubno), where they captured an important Russian position in two costly moonlight assaults.

Trumpeter of Croatian Hussar Regt, 1813. He is shown in the sky-blue dolman, and an iron-grey pelisse with Imperial livery lacing. Note his hussar busby with red-over-white-over-blue plume, and grey trousers with a long strap under his boot. In this sketch the buff facings are shown as yellow, including the busby bag. (R.Forthoffer, courtesy Umhey)

After marching to Moscow, the regiment fought during the retreat at Krasnoi on 18 November, suffering further heavy losses: on just one day nine officers were killed and 23 wounded. The survivors participated in the battle of the Beresina, but were no longer a cohesive unit. The other part of the regiment, which had stayed in the rear of the Grande Armée, took part in fighting during the retreat from Smorgony to Vilna from 3 to 11 December, in which it suffered badly: 23 officers were casualties, and just a handful of men reached safety.

The depot battalion was expanded and attached to Marshal Oudinot's corps in Germany in 1813 as part of Gen de Villeret's division, with which it fought at Gross-Beeren and Dennewitz in the late summer (losing eight officers in the latter action). Also weakened by desertion, the battalion fought at the battle of Leipzig in the 13th Division (Guillemont) of Gen Reynier's VII Corps; five officers including *Chef de bataillon* Aubert were wounded. The wreckage of the battalion retreated into France, where the Illyrian Regt was formally disbanded on 17 November 1813; the survivors were sent to Corsica to join the 2nd Colonial Battalion.

Marshal Marmont had proposed that the **uniform** and equipment should be the same as those of French light infantry, which would be a mark of honour and would help assimilate the Illyrian Regt into the French Army. Napoleon refused, wishing to avoid any confusion between French and foreign units. He ordered that the Illyrians be easily distinguishable by 'swallow's nest' shoulder wings on the French light infantry pattern blue jacket, faced scarlet on the collar and pointed cuffs. This 'swallow's nest' was probably red (although there are suggestions that it was blue), and was definitely piped white, as were the collar, cuffs and turn-backs. The white buttons were inscribed *'Empire francais'* surrounding *'Régiment d'Illyrie'*. The regiment is said to have been in rags by November 1813, most men lacking shoes and unable to march. There is no evidence that the Illyrian Regt ever received an Eagle or any other standard.

Croatian Hussar Regiment

After suffering the almost complete destruction of his cavalry in the Russian campaign, Napoleon welcomed Governor-General Bertrand's proposal of 15 February 1813 to revive the former 18th century Grenzer hussar units in the Illyrian Provinces. Bertrand believed (correctly) that the Croats' long experience of small-scale frontier warfare made them good riders who could be organized and trained quickly. Each of the Frontier Regiments was to finance and supply a troop of 100 hussars and their horses which – together with officers, NCOs and trumpeters –

Harambassa of Serezaners in Croatia, dressed in a green coat richly decorated with silver rings; a red waistcoat decorated to resemble a hussar dolman; blue trousers, loose in the thigh and tighter under the knees; colourful home made gaiters, and soft leather *Opanke* shoes. His red cap is decorated with a wide embroidered band and feathers, and his neck stock is black. His sabre is of the *karabela* type with a bird-head pommel. In the background are Serezaners mounted on small Bosnian ponies with Turkish-style horse furniture. (F.Jaschke, CHM)

(continued on page 33)

1806–08
1: Voltigeur, Royal Istrian Bn; Kopar, 1807
2: Carabinier, 2nd Dalmatian Bn; Venice, 1806
3: Chasseur, Royal Dalmatian Legion; Dalmatia, 1806–08

A

ILLYRIAN CHASSEURS 1810–13
1: Chasseur, 4th Regiment
2: Sergeant *porte-fanion*, 1st Bn, 3rd Regiment
3: *Chef de bataillon*, 6th Regiment
4: Administrative staff captain

B

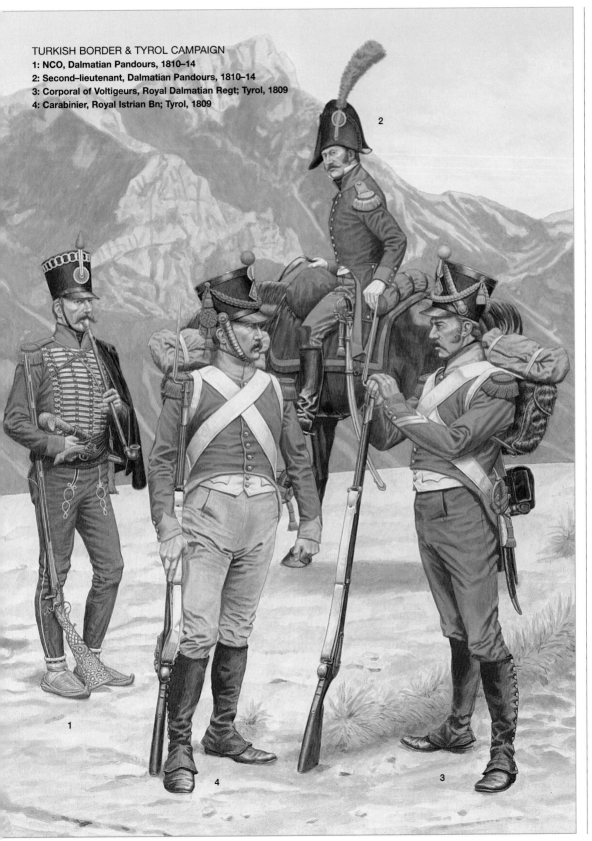

TURKISH BORDER & TYROL CAMPAIGN
1: NCO, Dalmatian Pandours, 1810–14
2: Second–lieutenant, Dalmatian Pandours, 1810–14
3: Corporal of Voltigeurs, Royal Dalmatian Regt; Tyrol, 1809
4: Carabinier, Royal Istrian Bn; Tyrol, 1809

C

CROATIAN PROVISIONAL REGIMENTS, 1812
1: Carabinier, 3rd Croatian Provisional Regt, Paris
2: Captain, Voltigeurs, 3rd Croatian Provisional Regt, Paris
3: Sergeant major, Voltigeurs, 1st Croatian Provisional Reg, Germany

D

RUSSIA 1812
1: Sergeant major, Carabiniers, Royal Dalmatian Regt
2: Drummer, Chasseurs, 1st Croatian Provisional Regt
3: Voltigeur, 3rd Croatian Provisional Regt
4: Lieutenant, Voltigeurs, Illyrian Regt

E

F

1812-14

1: *Harambassa*, Serezaners; Military Croatia, 1812
2: Chasseur, Illyrian Regt; Germany, 1813
3: Carabinier, 2nd Croatian Provisional Regt; Germany, 1813

CROATIAN HUSSARS & PIONEERS
1: Sergeant, Croatian Hussar Regt; Karlovac, 1813
2: Captain, Croatian Hussar Regt; Italy, 1813
3: Pioneer, Croatian Pioneers Bn; Bourges, France, 1814

G

IONIAN ISLANDS
1: Private, Albanian Regt, 1808–14
2: Officer, Albanian Regt, 1808–14
3: Chasseur, Septinsular Bn, 1808–12

would be consolidated into a regiment organized in three squadrons of two troops each. The horses had to be delivered with full equipment, and each rider had to be provided with stable dress and full kit for caring for his horse. All the citizens and towns of the Illyrian Provinces were ordered to display their loyalty by contributing money or horses and equipment; Bertrand himself provided 50 fully equipped horses. All voluntary contributions went towards the cost of 500 francs for a fully equipped horse and 2,000 francs for a fully equipped rider.

Napoleon's decree of 23 February 1813 created the Croatian Hussar Regiment (*Régiment de hussards croates*), which was assembled on 5 March at Karlovac under Bertrand's ADC, LtCol Bernard Pruès. So many men volunteered that a week later, instead of forming a second regiment as Bertrand advised, Napoleon amended his original decree to expand the regiment to six squadrons organized on the usual French hussar model. The staff of 21 comprised a colonel, two lieutenant-colonels, six *chefs d'escadron*, three adjutant-majors, a quartermaster, two accountants, a surgeon-major, two surgeons and three surgeon's assistants, plus 15 NCOs (six dismounted): three NCO adjutants, a veterinary and two assistants, three regimental trumpeters, a tailor, a saddler, three armourers and a cobbler. All the men and company officers came from the regiments of Illyrian Chasseurs (see above), while the staff were primarily cavalrymen from many mounted units, who were promoted on transfer. Bertrand himself was rewarded with command of IV Corps of the Grande Armée, which the Croatian Hussar Regt was ordered to join in Germany in April 1813; but it never did, since it was not yet fully equipped.

Nevertheless, together with 1,000 soldiers of the 4th Illyrian Chasseurs, some 220 of the Hussars successfully repulsed a cross-border raid by Ottoman Bosnian and Turkish troops after they had captured the key fortress of Cetin and massacred its garrison. Weaponry was in short supply, so the Hussars used whatever was available – all kinds of local sabres, pistols, muskets, and even ancient halberds which gave some of them the appearance of medieval mercenaries. They were also short of a number of officers, riding instructors, veterinaries and trumpeters. They performed well, however, despite their patchy knowledge of some basic manoeuvres. When the Minister of War permitted all native Frenchmen in the Illyrian Chasseurs regiments to join the Hussar regiment, the official establishment – 69 officers, 1,515 NCOs and men with 1,509 horses – was quickly reached on 2 August. However, Austria's declaration of war rendered the Croat element unreliable and prone to desertion.

The regiment was sent first to Italy, where 500 of the most reliable men formed a provisional advance guard, and took part in the autumn campaign with the Army of Italy. The rest were sent to Lyon in France for additional training; and a provisional detachment fought in the Tyrol, suffering one officer casualty in skirmishing on 15 August. At the end of September 200 Hussars joined 50 Chasseurs of the 19th Regt

Two Serezaners from the Croatian Military Border, dressed in white shirts with loose sleeves (note zig-zag red upper bands); richly decorated red waistcoats; red sashes with yellow decoration; tight blue breeches (note rear detail, left); colourful gaiter/socks and leather *Opanken*. One red cap has an embroidered decorative band; the man at left seems to have used his as a scarf. Their long muskets are shown with brass-covered butts; pistols and *yataghans* are tucked into the sash at the front; a small knife and two metal cartridge boxes are belted at the back. In the background is a large Chardak guardhouse.

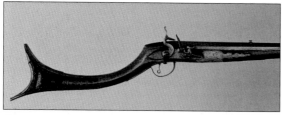

A

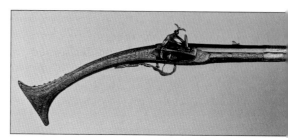

B

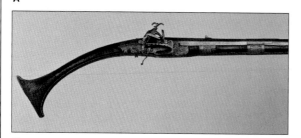

C

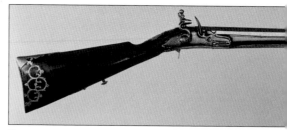

D

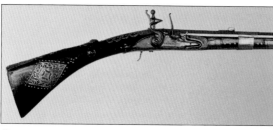

E

There were many varieties of Balkan guns, all decorated, and usually with long barrels of small calibre, which gave good accuracy. They are differentiated by the shape or decorative style of the stock.
(A) *Rašak*, produced in Bosnia and Herzegovina from the end of the 18th to the mid-19th century, and often mentioned in epic folksongs. (B) *Tančica, arnautka* or *krdžalinka*, produced in Kosovo, Šarplanina, western Macedonia and northern Albania, mid-18th century to 1870s, and exported to other parts of the border regions and Ottoman Empire. (C) Type of *tančica* produced in Boka Kotorska (Cattaro) and termed *šarajlija* because of the decorative 'scribbling'. (D) *Likas schtuz*, made up from parts of old military or hunting weapons – both smooth bore and rifled – and only modestly decorated. (E) Typical Dalmatian gun made up, stocked and decorated by local craftsmen from imported Italian barrels and locks. (CHM)

in a long-range reconnaissance near Garrets, sustaining a few casualties and losing 20 prisoners; but during the night of 4 October they deserted en masse. The remains of the unit were then disbanded and sent home, or to Lyon, where they arrived in October. This remnant was now just 657 strong, so local Frenchmen were recruited to bring the unit back up to full establishment.

A few weeks later, however, a decree of 25 November 1813 ordered the disbandment of all foreign regiments. The very next day Gen Corbineau arrived with Napoleon's order to disarm the 1,276 men of the regiment. The Hussars were stripped of much of their equipment: 639 of their horses were passed to the 31er Chasseurs à Cheval and 208 to the 1er Hussards, 1,232 carbines, 1,249 sabres and 469 bayonets were placed in the Lyon arsenal, and the unit was formally disbanded on 23 January 1814. All French citizens were sent to the 4e Dragons, while some Croatian officers with particularly strong connections to France were allowed to petition the Minister of War for active employment in other cavalry regiments.

The Croatian Hussar Regiment's **uniform**, equipment and horse-furniture were officially of the French pattern. General Bertrand's order of 11 February 1813 described its features, which remained largely unchanged throughout the Croatian Hussars' brief existence. He ordered the purchase of 657 sets of horse furniture including saddle covers; and 657 uniforms comprising a pair of hussar boots with steel spurs, iron-grey overalls with leather reinforcements, sky-blue dolmans with light buff *(chamoise)* collar and cuffs, pelisses, black neck stocks, iron-grey overcoats, haversacks and undress caps. The black felt shakos had white metal chin scales; a lozenge plate bearing either the words '1er Régiment d'hussards croates' or simply '1'; and a company-colour pompon. Napoleon's quick rejection of a proposal for a second Croatian hussar regiment suggests that the regimental number also disappeared.

Bertrand's decree is silent about the colour of the pelisse, but he had already ordered 657 in iron-grey. When Napoleon prescribed a sky-blue pelisse, there was a brief period of confusion: Col Pruès suggested that the grey pelisses which had already been made should be turned into stable jackets and the new colour issued, and the Minister of War Direction, Count Cessac, agreed; but Napoleon balked at the unnecessary expense, and on 2 July 1813 formally authorized the grey pelisse – this was trimmed with black lambskin. Like the breeches and leather-reinforced overalls the pelisse was in a shade described as iron-grey or 'goat hair grey'. The corded decoration on the dolman and breeches was white; the buttons were pewter, and the waist sash was white with crimson barrelling. The whitened leather cross belt/sling worn over the left shoulder supported a black cartridge box and the carbine. The black hussar boots were edged white, with a tassel on the V-cut front. The cloak and valise were iron-grey; the saddle cover was of black sheepskin with buff 'wolf-tooth' edging. A shortage of weapons restricted the hussars' armament to sabres and carbines, as no pistols were issued. Officially, though probably not in reality, regimental trumpeters were to wear the 1812 pattern 'Imperial Livery', or a uniform of reversed colours – a light buff dolman with sky-blue collar and cuffs. There is no evidence that the Hussars ever received a standard.

(Left to right) *Schiavona* broadsword, as produced and used in Dalmatia from the 16th century, this one being fitted with the three-bar style of basket hilt seen in the 18th/19th centuries; a Dalmatian sabre, a local version of the Austrian hussar sabre, used in the 18th century by Dalmatian mercenaries, infantry officers and mounted troops in Venetian service; and an Albanian-Dalmatian sword, used mostly by Albanian mercenaries in Venetian service, and as personal weapons throughout Dalmatia and Albania from the 16th to the early 19th century. (Aralica)

Pioneers

A battalion of *Pionniers Croates,* composed of five companies, was created from the remaining Croatian personnel of the disbanded Croatian Hussar Regt – one of various Foreign Pioneer Battalions raised in late 1813. After they were re-equipped at Nevers on 31 December, the battalion was sent to Bourges in France under *Chef d'escadron* Pavlica. After Napoleon's abdication in April 1814 the battalion was disbanded and the remnants were repatriated to their Frontier homes. When they arrived in Bourges, this battalion were kitted out from the stores of the *Pionniers blancs*, another foreign corps of the French Army, but most of the former Hussars retained their old uniforms.

Serezaners

The Serezaners had been raised by the Austrians from Bosnian refugees in the 1790s, when units of 200 men were attached to each of the six Grenzer regiments. Their main functions were to act as scouts in wartime and to provide additional patrols and cross-border raiding parties along the Frontier, as well as serving as couriers, when they often rode small ponies. When the French took over these regiments they continued to employ the Serezaners in the same way, under direction of the colonel and day-to-day command of their own NCOs, who retained their old Bosnian titles: *oberbassa* or *harambassa* (sergeant major), *unterbassa* (sergeant) and *vicebassa* (corporal).

The Serezaners did not wear a **uniform**, but retained traditional local costume: loose blue or white shirts and blue or red waistcoats, decorated with silver rings and buttons; small red caps worn in summer were replaced in cold weather by a larger pointed red hat with a colourful embroidered white band around it. Their trousers were usually dark blue, white or brown in the loose Croatian style (*benevrake*); light blue Hungarian and wide Turkish-style trousers were also worn, all usually tied just below the knees, above local soft leather shoes or *Opanke* sandals, with colourful embroidered woollen home-made gaiters. Over the shirt and waistcoat they might wear a brown, blue or green jacket or longer coat (*gunjac*), often trimmed in red. They were most recognisable by their hooded red cloaks, made famous by the 18th century Balkan irregulars. Their armament included various types of richly decorated Balkan pistols, swords and knives, the former carried in the pockets of a wide brown or red leather waistbelt (*bensilah*), which was usually decorated with small lead balls. Guns, which were often slung across the back, were sometimes of the short-barrelled Balkan types like the *likas schtuz* (carbine), but more usually had a long barrel in the styles known as *čibuklija, paragun* and *sheshana*. NCOs also carried sabres of Turkish *kilij* or Polish *karabela* types. A last essential piece of equipment was the long wooden pipe and smoking set.

National Guard

The first **Garde nationale** unit was raised by Gen Lauriston from the inhabitants of Dubrovnik in 1806, to help him defend the city from the Russians and Montenegrins. In 1809 there were four battalions of National Guard, located at Zadar, Dubrovnik (two battalions), and Kotor to strengthen the defence of these towns and their harbours after the French troops had left for the campaign against Austria. In the following years the Guard was considerably expanded, especially after the French troops in the Provinces were reduced to one division, and in 1811 it numbered around 10,000 men. It was formed in all the towns and ports on the Adriatic coast and islands, individual companies being raised from local populations under the command of prominent citizens. The ports, which had gun batteries, raised coastal guard artillery companies (*Compagnia di cannonieri guarda costa*) under the command of French instructors, to resist the regular raids by British

The seven Ionian Islands of Corfu, Paxos, Santa-Maura, Ithaca, Cephalonia, Zante and Cerigo.

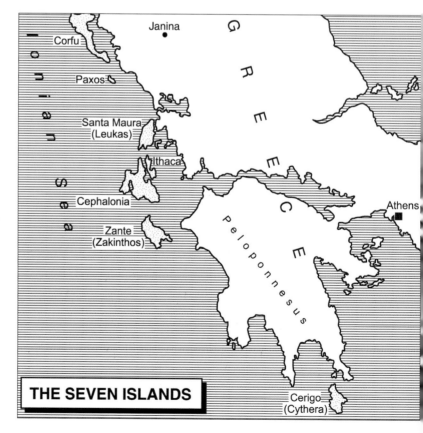

THE SEVEN ISLANDS

vessels. However, they were only permitted to fire on the British if they were trying to land or rob the boats in the harbour. It seems that the National Guard was very popular with the inhabitants: Marshal Marmont noted that service was regarded as an honour and many enlisted willingly – he had never seen a better National Guard anywhere. Their military prowess did not live up to his hopes, however; although some British raids were repelled, more often the Guard units broke up and scattered.

These Guardsmen were provided only with weapons and food on active duty and were only paid when away from their home towns. The wealthy paid for their **uniforms** themselves, while a fund was organized in each company to purchase uniforms for the poorer men. The French-style uniform was similar to that of line infantry, but the costs meant that most men wore local civilian costume. Some districts in Istria managed to purchase uniforms for their units in the Bavarian light infantry style, consisting of a green jacket with black collar, green breeches and black gaiters; cuffs and piping were yellow, as was the shako pompon above the French cockade. As a distinction the National Guard of Kopar (Coppar) had epaulettes. The artillerymen wore the same uniform except that the cuffs, epaulettes, piping and pompon were red. The Provincial authorities were supposed to pay for a musket and bayonet for each man, but many used their own small calibre Balkan-style guns, especially in Dalmatia. Some also carried pistols and swords, usually of the old *Schiavona* type with a characteristic basket hilt, which were in use from the 17th to mid-19th century, or 18th century Dalmatian sabres. Such old weaponry was very common on the eastern Adriatic coast.

Although of a later date, this Turkish janissary captain from Janina, 1831, is dressed in the style preferred by clan chiefs and high-ranking officers of Albanian and Ionian Islands units earlier in the century. The richly decorated scarlet waistcoat and jacket are worn under a blue cloak edged red. His weaponry is the usual pair of entirely decorated pistols with straight butts, which were carried in a red waistbelt; his main status symbol is the long *yataghan*. Note the gold embroidery on his scarlet turban; and the decorated metal leg protection. (Umhey)

IONIAN/SEVEN ISLANDS CORPS

Les troupes Septinsulaire were composed mostly of the native population, a mix of Greeks, Albanians and Italians; these were augmented by 'Illyrians', most of whom were Dalmatians enlisted when these units were garrisoned on the mainland coast. They were led by a mixture of French officers and NCOs together with assorted adventurers from various nations. All were disbanded in 1814.

Albanian Regiment

The *Régiment albanais* had its origins in a Venetian regiment transferred into French service in 1797, together with an Albanian militia raised by the Russians in 1799, which passed to the French when they recovered the Ionian Islands in 1807. On 12 October that year Napoleon approved the recruitment of about 3,000 Albanians, most of whom were refugees from the harsh rule of the local Ottoman governor of the Albanian coast, Ali-pasha of Janina. The combined force was organized as the Albanian Regiment on 12 December 1807, with three battalions each comprising a staff and nine companies. Despite additional recruitment among local Greeks, Italians and Dalmatian communities, it never reached its official establishment of 3,254. A battalion of **Greek Foot Chasseurs**   37

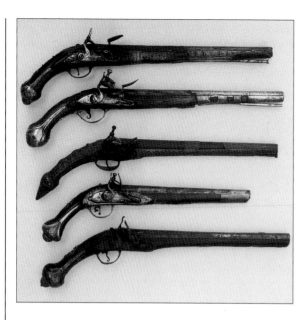

The top two pistols are Dalmatian, from the 18th/19th century: (top) this has a 17th or 18th century Italian barrel and a re-used Brescia lock; (second) this has a Brescia barrel and mechanism, which is falsely engraved 'London', since London-made weapons were highly prized in the western Balkans. The lower three weapons are: (third) a 'rat-tail' pistol or *silja*, widely used in Dalmatia, Albania, Greece and Bulgaria, this example being typical of Konavle, Herzegovina and Kosovo; (fourth) a pistol characteristic of rural parts of Military Croatia and northern Dalmatia, incorporating features copied from Austrian weapons such as the *capucine*, with the muzzle band resembling the 1798 pattern pistol; and (bottom) a high quality pistol from Bosnia and Herzegovina as produced in Sarajevo and Foča – precision-made, but not as decoratively ornamented as many examples. (Aralica)

(Chasseurs à pied Grecs), also known as **Pandours de Albanie** was raised by the French under an order of 10 March 1808 from Albanian and Greek refugees discovered on the Ionian Islands after the treaty of Tilsit. Its 951 men were divided into eight companies, three being designated as elite. The two units were combined into a single **Albanian Regiment** on 1 July 1809, organized on the French model into six battalions, totalling 160 officers and 2,934 men. Each battalion was composed of one elite and five fusilier companies.

The regiment was scattered in various garrisons across the Ionian Islands. As all the men were volunteers and could leave when they wished, discipline was more relaxed – even officers would regularly travel to the mainland to deal with feuding relatives or to rustle sheep for the mess table. Blood feuds played a central part in Albanian culture, and inter-family and ethnic hostility made for poor unit cohesion and fighting spirit, which resulted in variable combat performance. The companies which garrisoned the islands of Zante, Cephalonia, and Ithaca in October 1809 fought valiantly until overwhelmed by superior British numbers; but in contrast, all 34 officers and 789 men of the battalion sent to take part in the defence of Saint-Maure deserted to the enemy en masse, except 13 who were languishing in jail. (Most of these men joined the Duke of York's Light Infantry raised by the British.)

The rest of the regiment stayed on Corfu, and saw no further combat. Desertion rates were always high; consequently the regiment was reorganized into a staff and two battalions on 6 November 1813, totalling 47 officers and 1,204 men – augmented unofficially by 1,036 women and children, 1,426 goats, 36 horses, a mule and a cow… Various proposals envisaged taking some men to Naples to join Joachim Murat's Royal Army, or adding 500 Albanians to Napoleon's Imperial Guard, but these came to nothing. (Three volunteer horsemen 'mounted, armed and equipped in the manner of their ancestors' did travel to Paris in 1813 for inspection by the Minister of War; their similarity to the Mamelukes led to them joining that Guard squadron during the 1814 campaign.) Following the French evacuation of the island of Corfu in 1814, the Albanian Regt was taken over by the British, but it quickly evaporated of its own accord, before being officially disbanded on 21 June 1814.

The men of all these units wore their local Albanian-style **costume**, described by Col Minot in a letter to the Minister of War: 'Their dress is very luxurious, with red wool beret with a gold tassel, sandals with thick soles, coloured gaiters, a tunic with a short skirt (*tunique fustanelle*), a short scarlet vest decorated with gold buttons with sleeves open to the elbow, a long red wool sash with gold tassels, and a thick goatskin cloak that is impermeable to rain and invaluable for bivouacking.' All were armed with one or two pistols, a yataghan and a Balkan Turkish-style small calibre gun with a long barrel. The pistols had an almost straight grip and were completely covered with brass or silver decoration. The yataghan was of characteristic 'Greek' ('Epyr'/ 'Cretan') style. The muskets, which were often also richly decorated, were known as *arnautka, šarajlija, rašak* and *roga* (see page 34).

Septinsular Battalion

The 'Seven Islands Battalion' (***Bataillon Septinsulaire***) was a six-company light infantry unit raised on 13 September 1807 from the men of a former Venetian regiment, who had then been in Russian pay. Each company's strength stood at about 150 men, who were to be recruited exclusively from the Ionian Islands population. In January 1808 the battalion was reorganized into nine companies and the number of soldiers reduced to 100 per company. Nevertheless, the battalion had constant problems with recruiting enough men, and resorted to filling its ranks with Austrian prisoners of war in 1809, and later with Dalmatians, Italians and Neapolitans while it was briefly stationed in Dalmatia. Another proposal to take in Spanish prisoners was rejected by Napoleon. The battalion was deployed in the defence of the Ionian Islands, but after the detachment under Col Piéris on Cephalonia surrendered to the British without firing a shot in 1809, Napoleon took the view that they did not justify their cost and the Septinsular Battalion was disbanded in 1812; the remnants were incorporated into the *Sapeurs Ioniens*.

The **uniform** was in French light infantry style, comprising a shako with a brass plate, plume and cords, a dark blue jacket (with epaulettes for elite companies), waistcoat and trousers, together with short black gaiters. The jacket was also lined in dark blue, although faced with

LEFT **Albanian officer dressed in green jacket and scarlet waistcoat, embroidered with gold; his long white shirt hangs like a kilt over his wide Turkish-style scarlet trousers tied just below the knees. (Umhey)**

RIGHT **Albanian soldier in a simple white shirt and short off-white jacket both embroidered in red, and a thick goatskin cloak. The French found the Albanian hairstyle – the head shaved in Asiatic style, leaving only a long scalplock – quite intimidating. (Umhey)**

This carabinier of the Septinsular Battalion wears a dark blue single-breasted jacket with sky-blue collar; the dark blue cuffs and sky-blue three-button cuff flaps are piped red, as are the trousers and the hussar-cut gaiters. The waistcoat is sky-blue; the epaulettes and all shako embellishments are red. E.Fieffe illustrates this type of soldier with sky-blue cuffs and flaps, dark blue waistcoat, undecorated trousers and white gaiters, and shows an all-red sabre knot. (Alsatian Manuscript, courtesy Umhey)

sky-blue on the collar and cuffs with the same colour piping. (However Forthoffer claims they had red facings.) Officers wore gold epaulettes and shako cords.

Ionian Mounted Chasseurs

A squadron of **Chasseurs à cheval ioniens** was created on the island of Corfu on 27 November 1807, but served on all the Ionian Islands. Its provisional form was one squadron of cavalry, but it was reduced to a single company of 128 officers and men on 13 December 1808. The unit was recruited from the natives, but some men of the 25e Chasseurs à cheval also joined them from the Kingdom of Naples, and the latter's uniform was adopted by all personnel. It consisted of a green jacket with dark red (*garance*) facings but with buttons bearing the inscription '*Chasseurs Ioniens*'. The unit was evacuated to France in 1814 with the rest of the French garrison of Corfu, and remnants were incorporated into the 6e Lanciers at Lyon.

The other Ionian units were two companies of Septinsular Artillery (**Artillerie Septinsulaire**) raised on 1 January 1808; a company of **Sapeurs Ioniens** formed on 7 August 1812 by combining the former 9th Company of White Pioneers (*Pionniers Blancs*) with the remnants of the Septinsular Battalion; the **Gendarmerie Septinsulaire**, probably one company strong; and the **Vétérans Septinsulaire/Ioniens**. All appear to have been organized and equipped in the same way as their French counterparts, but were probably dressed in national costume. All served sporadically on the Dalmatian coast as well as the islands, and all were disbanded in 1814.

FOREIGN TROOPS IN THE ILLYRIAN PROVINCES

The **Oriental Chasseurs** (*Chasseurs d'Orient*) originated in the local volunteer units raised by the French from the Greeks, Turks, Copts and Syrians in the Middle East during Napoleon's 1798–99 campaign. These troops were shipped back to Marseille after Egypt was evacuated in 1801, and organized into a light unit by an order of 7 January 1802. The eight companies, including one each of carabiniers and artillerymen, totalled just 339 men. Despite a steady stream of desertions, an order of 10 September 1802 directed the battalion to be expanded to 1,000 men organized into a staff and ten companies, but it never numbered more than 400. Nevertheless, when assigned to Gen Molitor's expedition to relieve Gen Lauriston besieged in Dubrovnik in 1806 by the Russians and Montenegrins, the unit distinguished themselves and earned three crosses of the Legion of Honour; but the price was heavy, total strength being reduced to 17 officers and 60 men by 20 November 1806.

After service in southern France and Italy, the battalion was transferred in 1809 to garrisons in Dalmatia and then Corfu, where it was attached to the Albanian Regiment. Despite additional local recruiting (an 1812 list includes 18 French, four Italians, one Neapolitan, one German, one Pole, one Hungarian, 17 Dalmatians, 14 Archipelago Greeks, 30 Ionian Greeks, one Serb and 15 Egyptians), the battalion's strength fell from 293 in 1810 to 96 in February 1813, when

French gunners instructing Greeks of the Septinsular Artillery. Although this unit is said to have worn the same uniforms as French line foot artillery, these Greeks are shown in their native costume, which is more likely. (P.Wagner, courtesy Umhey)

the unit was shipped from Corfu to Ancona in Italy. It continued to fight alongside the French until 1814, when it was again transferred to Marseille. All non-French were sent to a refugee depot, and the battalion was officially disbanded on 24 September 1814 at Lyon. The **uniform**, equipment and armament of the Middle Eastern Chasseurs were the same as those of the French light infantry.

* * *

Several **French and Italian units** served in Illyria from 1806 to 1813. The first were the French 5e, 23e, 79e and 81e de Ligne from Gen Molitor's division, which occupied the territories acquired under the Treaty of Pressburg early in 1806. Additional troops were required after the Russians attacked the region and incited local rebellions. The French 8e and 18e Léger, 11e and 60e de Ligne arrived the same year, together with the 24e Chasseurs à cheval, four companies of 8e and one company of 2e Régiments d'artillerie à pied, two companies of Pioneers, two battalions of the Italian Royal Guard, two Italian artillery companies, and the Bersaglieri di Brescia.

For the campaign of 1809 against Austria, a so-called 'Army of Dalmatia' under Marmont's command was formed from these troops, which fought its way through Croatia to join Napoleon's main forces at Vienna. The army was composed of two divisions accompanied by 12 guns; the division of Gen Montrichard comprised the 18e Léger and the 5e, 79e, and 81e de Ligne, and that of Gen Clausel the 8e Léger, 11e and 23e de Ligne, and 24e Chasseurs à cheval. The 60e de Ligne, the 1st Bn of the 3rd Italian Light Infantry (former Bersaglieri di Brescia), the Pioneers, and the rest of the gunners remained garrisoned in Dalmatia.

After the campaign this army returned to the now extended French possessions, but was reduced to one division in 1811. Partly for financial reasons, but more because Napoleon needed the French troops elsewhere, the 8e and 18e Léger and the 5e, 60e and 81e de Ligne left for Spain. Later the 8e and 18e Léger and 24e

French brass drum, with painted white diamonds around the red wooden hoops. The number '1' is engraved into the brass bracket holding the tensioning hook. (MS)

On 28 October 1956, at the *Hôtel National des Invalides* in Paris, a memorial plaque honouring all Croatian soldiers in French service during the Napoleonic Wars was unveiled and dedicated by the French government. The inscription reads: 'In memory of the Croat Regiments which, [fighting] under the French flag, shared in the glory of the French Army'.

Chasseurs à cheval were sent to Russia in 1812, together with 1st Bn, 3rd Italian Light Infantry. The 11e and 23e de Ligne joined the army in Germany in 1813, so that only four French battalions (apparently of the 79e de Ligne), a few hundred French and Italian gunners and French gendarmes were left in the Provinces when the Austrians invaded. Two French units augmented the Ionian Islands garrisons – the 14e Léger and 6e de Ligne – together with a few platoons from the 25e Chasseurs à cheval.

Finally, even the British raised a Croatian battalion. Formed on the island of Vis (Lissa) in 1812 from deserters and prisoners, it participated in the capture of the south Dalmatian ports of Slano, Herceg-Novi, Cavtat, and Ston by the Royal Navy. Apparently no special dress was issued, but the old uniforms and civilian clothes were worn until the unit was disbanded at the end of the campaign.

BIBLIOGRAPHY & FURTHER READING

Only a few general survey books in English refer to this theatre of Napoleon's wars: Elting, *Swords Around a Throne* (1988), especially Chapter XVIII; Rothenberg, *The Military Border in Croatia 1740–1881* (1966). Three books cover the organization, history and uniforms of some Balkan units: Dempsey, *Napoleon's Mercenaries, Foreign Units in the French Army Under the Consulate and Empire, 1799 to 1814* (2002); Chartrand, *Napoleon's Army* (1996); and Nafziger, *Régiments Hors de Ligne (Foreign Regiments)*, Volume 5 of *The French Army, Royal, Republican, Imperial, 1792–1815* (1997).

Several works in French, German and Italian cover this subject: Fieffe, *Histoire des troupes étrangers au service de France depuis leur origine jusqu'a nos jours* (1854) is a general study of all French foreign units through history; *Mémoires du duc de Raguse de 1792 à 1832* (1857) – the memoirs of Marshal Marmont, first governor of the Illyrian Provinces; Vaniček, *Specialgeschichte der Militärgrenze* (1875) covers the organization of the Military Border under Austrian rule; Boppe, Paul, *La Croatie Militaire 1809–1813* (1900) deals with the part of the Military Border (Military Croatia) and its units under French rule. L'Invalide, 'Les Hussards Croates and Les Régiments Croates et Leur Uniformes (1809–14)' in *La Giberne*, Vol XII (1910–11), 129–39, 139–143 & 149–58, is a good article on these units, useful in conjunction with Knötel's article 'Die Uniformierung der Kroaten in den Feldzugen 1812 u.1813' in *Die Mölkerbastei*, Vol 3 (1951). Forthoffer, Roger, *Soldats du temps jadis: France 1805–15 – Le 1er, 2e, 3e & 4e Régiments étrangers (Fiches documentaires 210–213, 215–229)* were privately published. Addobatti, *Il Regimento Reale Dalmata* (1899), covers the Royal Dalmatian Regt in a diary style; Boppe, *La Régiment Albanais 1807–1814* (1902), deals with the history of the Albanian Regt; Baeyens, Jacques, *Les Francais à Corfou* (1973) includes both Albanian and French/foreign units on the Ionian islands. Jean-Pierre Perconte's web site about Napoleon's Italian Troops includes Dalmatian units and the Istrian Battalion – www.histunif.com.

HE PLATES

A1: *Voltigeur*, Royal Istrian Battalion; Kopar, 1807

The black *corsehut,* with the enlarged left brim turned up, was popular among central European light infantry at this time. The uniform consists of a single-breasted green jacket with sky-blue facings and green epaulettes. The leatherwork was white, but some reconstructions show it as black.

A2: *Carabinier*, 2nd Dalmatian Battalion; Venice, 1806

The *corsehut* which replaced the Austrian leather helmet is decorated only with the Italian tricolour cockade fastened with a white loop. The carabinier company were distinguished by their red pompons, epaulettes and sword knots. The 2nd Battalion, often referred to as the Dalmatian Marine Battalion (*Batallion dalmate de la Marine*) because of its regular service on Italian Navy vessels, was distinguished from the 1st only by sky-blue breeches. Both battalions had green single-breasted jackets with red facings, and a waistcoat cut in the Austrian style.

A3: *Chasseur*, Royal Dalmatian Legion; Dalmatia, 1806–08

The Dalmatian Legion's uniforms differed from those of the Dalmatian battalions only by the white waistcoat and green breeches. The chasseurs initially wore soft leather *Opanke* shoes and colourful woollen socks/gaiters, which were replaced later by regulation French black shoes and gaiters.

B1: *Chasseur*, 4th Regiment of Illyrian Chasseurs, 1810–13

An unsuccessful attempt to dye the Austrian brown jacket blue has turned it almost black; it was permitted to be worn until new uniforms could be produced, but with new facing colours (orange for the 4th Regiment). The white *Hausmontur* trousers and black Hungarian boots also remained in use, along with a peaked *Klobuk* with the French cockade added. Although light troops, Illyrian Chasseurs never received the standard light infantry sabres, so they continued to carry just a bayonet scabbard on the white leather belt over the right shoulder.

Although the carabinier of the Dalmatian Regt (left) is correctly illustrated in a green uniform with red facings and decorations and a white waistcoat, the carabinier (centre) – supposedly from the 1st Illyrian Regt – wears a white uniform which seems to be imaginary. The soldier (right) – supposedly from the 2nd Illyrian Regt – is probably an Illyrian, dressed in the regular French light infantry uniform. There was only one 'Illyrian Regt', and the artist has presumably confused it with the six regiments of Illyrian Chasseurs. The large, white-piped, scarlet shoulder straps are probably meant to be the 'swallow's nests' which the Chasseurs actually wore on the shoulder as a distinction from French regiments. (A.de Valmont, Cliché BNFP)

The surviving *fanion* of the 1st Bn, 3rd Regt of Illyrian Chasseurs (see Plate B) was made of wool, measuring 107x100cm (42x39in), and was flown on a leather-covered staff 291.5cm (9ft 6in) long. The white flag bears the diagonal inscription '3eme. Illyrien. 1eme Bon [Bataillon]'. (MHMV)

B2: Sergeant *porte-fanion*, 1st Battalion, 3rd Regiment of Illyrian Chasseurs, 1810–13
This NCO wears the former Austrian white pre-1808 infantry jacket *(Feldmontur)* dyed blue, which produced a better result than attempts to dye brown jackets; he has Hungarian-style light blue breeches, and short black gaiters cut to resemble hussar boots with white tape edging and small tassels. The sergeant's chevron on his forearms is in silver lace. As well as his musket he is armed with an infantry sabre with a white sword knot. The white *fanion* was prescribed by regulations for regimental 1st Battalions.

B3: *Chef de bataillon,* 6th Regiment of Illyrian Chasseurs, 1810–13
Officers were expected to purchase their own uniforms and were probably the only troops to have the regulation uniform. The 'national blue' uniform is an interesting mixture of a basic Austrian-style jacket or sometimes a French-style *surtout* with additions of French origin such as epaulettes and a gorget. The officer has a new 1810 model shako with red plume as prescribed for his rank, and a tricolour cockade worn instead of a shako plate. Note the popular style of green waist belt and sabre frog laced with silver; hussar-style boots reinforce the light cavalry appearance greatly appreciated by the Croat regiments.

B4: Administrative staff captain, Illyrian Chasseurs, 1810–13
The staff officers were the only administrative officers of Illyrian regiments who wore white trousers and a waistcoat, together with the usual blue *habit*, with collar, cuffs and turn-backs of the same colour. Epaulettes, sword furniture, sword knot and hat decoration were gold, as were the buttons bearing the imperial eagle. The distinctions of the staff officer were the same as in the French Army.

C1: NCO, Dalmatian Pandours, 1810–14
His dress is a mixture of uniform and native dress based on both infantry and cavalry styles: a hussar-style blue dolman with white buttons and decoration, with a red collar, cuffs and epaulettes; tight blue breeches with white stripes and knots; a wide red belt holding a pistol and a yataghan; and soft leather Opanke shoes with home made wool gaiters. The regulation shako is black with a decorated top band, a red pompon and a cockade.

C2: Second-lieutenant, Dalmatian Pandours, 1810–14
This officer's uniform consists of a black cocked hat with a tricolour cockade attached by a silver loop, and a tall red plume. His blue *habit,* faced red at collar, cuffs and turn-backs, has silver buttons; the epaulette on the left shoulder and contre-epaulette on the right are of silver bullion. The tight red breeches have silver lace side stripes and thigh knots.

C3: Corporal of *Voltigeurs*, Royal Dalmatian Regiment; Tyrol, 1809
The soldiers of the Royal Dalmatian Regiment adopted the uniform of the former Royal Dalmatian Legion, but replaced the *corsehut* with a French-style shako. On the yellow metal diamond-shaped plate the initials below the Iron Crown of Lombardy were changed from 'LRD' to 'RRD'. Voltigeurs were distinguished by yellow shako cords and pompon together with green epaulettes and sword knot.

C4: *Carabinier*, Royal Istrian Battalion; Tyrol, 1809
The new French-style shako had red cords and pompon for the carabinier company, with 'BRI' below the Lombard crown on a brass diamond plate. Another distinction for the carabiniers was a red sword knot, although this man is still dressed in an Austrian uniform with French distinctions.

D1: *Carabinier*, 3rd Croatian Provisional Regiment; Paris, 1812
During their stay in Paris soldiers of the 3rd Regt were dressed in a new green uniform, but cut in the old light infantry style. The jacket had a yellow collar and pointed cuffs and piped lapels, and they probably wore green grenades on the turn-backs. They also had a characteristic

OPPOSITE **Pandour and Serezaner equipment. (Top to bottom:) Cartridge boxes; the first three, from western Bosnia and Ravni Kotari – the hinterland of Zadar – are made of leather decorated with small lead studs, while the other two are made of brass and come from inland Dalmatia (Zagora); (below) the richly ornamented silver box is of Turkish origin; the two small brass boxes to its left are for animal fat and scrap metal for weapon maintenance. Some characteristic small knives: that between the cartridge boxes, from Sinj, has a brass grip decorated with a snake stuck in a horse's mane, a favourite symbol in Balkan epic songs. (Below left) two small folding knives *(britule),* and (right) a typical Bosnian *bichaj*. (Bottom right) Balkan pistols usually lacked their own ramrod, so the man carried a multi purpose rod such as these two, known as *Arbija*, of mixed metal and wood construction. Pipe-smoking was widely enjoyed, and the kit included flint, a steel striker and tinder as well as the small socketed pipe bowl (bottom left). (Aralica)** ellow side-stripe down their trouser seams. The collar probably did not have the additional piping and patch suggested in some reconstructions (e.g. page 15). The shako has a red plume above the pompon and red side chevrons, which together with the red epaulettes and sword knot were the distinctions for carabiniers.

2: Captain of *Voltigeurs*, 3rd Croatian Provisional Regiment; Paris, 1812
The officers also received new green uniforms, but they sometimes changed the colour of the waistcoat to yellow or green as shown here. Although the shako usually bore a white metal eagle plate displaying the regimental number, this officer has a diamond-shaped plate with a hunting horn motif; together with his yellow plume, this indicates that he is the captain of the voltigeur company – note also his light infantry sabre.

3: Sergeant major of *Voltigeurs*, 1st Croatian Provisional Regiment; Germany, 1812
The soldiers of the 1st Regt probably also received the new green uniforms when they arrived in Germany on their way to the Russian campaign. As distinctions voltigeurs had a yellow-tipped red plume and a yellow pompon, top band and side chevrons, together with a yellow sword knot and yellow epaulettes fringed green. When a change of the weapon was requested the voltigeurs probably received the *An IX/XIII* Dragoon musket, widely used by the light infantry instead of the longer, heavier infantry model. Note the silver double rank chevrons above his cuffs.

E1: Sergeant major of *Carabiniers*, Royal Dalmatian Regiment; Russia, 1812
This sergeant major of the elite company displays the standard campaign equipment; he is wearing long white overall trousers instead of breeches, and a linen shako cover with a separate pompon cover. His plume also has its own linen cover, and is tied to his sabre scabbard by the shako cords, as was common on campaign.

E2: Drummer of *Chasseurs*, 1st Croatian Provisional Regiment, Russia, 1812
This *tambour* is shown wearing a *pokalem* forage cap, although the Provisional Regiments may equally have been issued with the older *bonnet de police* pattern. Both patterns were carried rolled and strapped under the cartridge box when not in use – see E1. At the front it bears the number not of the Provisional Regt but of his parent regiment of Chasseurs Illyriens; a red grenade was substituted for carabiniers and a yellow horn for voltigeurs. Note the distinctive white summer trousers with a yellow side-stripe, and the Imperial Livery lace in alternate green and yellow

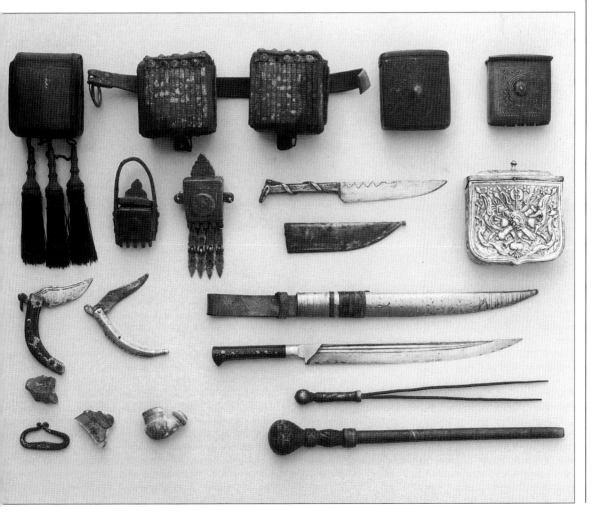

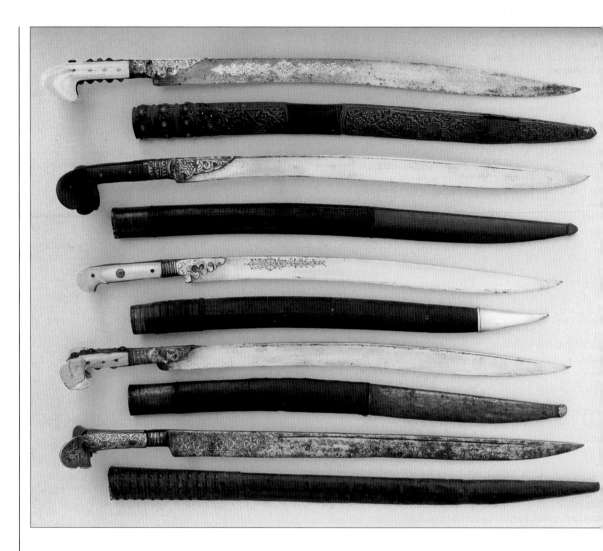

segments, the latter decorated alternately with an eagle and a crowned 'N' in green. Having no previous elaborate drummer uniforms, the Croat units could incorporate this new style more quickly than their French counterparts.

E3: *Voltigeur*, 3rd Croatian Provisional Regiment; Russia, 1812

For his comfort in the summer heat this light company soldier has rolled his trouser cuffs, revealing their white lining. The flap of his cartridge box is covered with white fabric, which probably had a painted black horn and regimental, battalion or company symbols. His shako is enclosed in a black oilskin, with the pompon left uncovered. The collar is shown with the sky-blue edging and patch reconstructed in Forthoffer's drawings. During the retreat of II Corps from Polotsk a whole company of voltigeurs was lost when the bridges were blown up too early.

E4: Lieutenant of *Voltigeurs*, Illyrian Regiment; Russia, 1812

This officer wears a bicorn and a single-breasted *surtout* with a scarlet collar, both these items being preferred on active service. White or blue long trousers, or even overalls of light cavalry style, were common on campaign instead of the breeches worn here. The bicorn, with the yellow voltigeur

pompon, was usually covered with oilskin or linen. On his waist belt he carries a curved sabre, in place of the regulation epée and shoulder belt, to emulate the light cavalry style.

F1: *Harambassa* of Serezaners; Military Croatia, 1812

In addition to the main weapon, a short musket (*Schtuz*), the Serezaners carried a pair of Balkan pistols, and a long Turkish knife (*yataghan*) with a white or black bone grip. A shorter *bichaj* knife was also tucked in the waist belt together with the pistol ramrod.

F2: *Chasseur*, Illyrian Regiment, 1813

Although in the uniform of French light infantry with scarlet facings, this chasseur is distinguished from his French colleagues by the scarlet 'swallow's nest' shoulder wings piped in white. Napoleon had specifically ordered this feature to ensure that French and foreign regiments could be instantly distinguished from one another.

F3: *Carabinier*, 2nd Croatian Provisional Regiment; Germany, 1813

The shortage of new uniforms led to the 2nd Croatian Provisional Regt being sent to the Grande Armée in their old

OPPOSITE A selection of *yataghan* knives:
(Top) Produced in Sarajevo, late 18th century, for a Turkish janissary *bassa* (NCO), this has a pommel of mammoth ivory, an Arabic inscription, and a scabbard decorated with silver studded with red stones. (Second) An ordinary soldier's weapon, c.1814–15, with a black pommel of water buffalo horn. (Third) Typical Cretan or Aegean *yataghan*, c.1795, as used by the inhabitants of the Greek islands and the coast, as well as sailors. (Fourth) Bosnian weapon from the early 19th century, obviously produced for the trade with Christian Military Croatia and Dalmatia, since it has no Islamic symbols; the pommel is of walrus ivory. (Bottom) Dalmatian *yataghan* with a straight blade, early 19th century; rough brass pommel cover decorated with foliate motifs, as produced in inland towns all over Dalmatia. (Aralica)

RIGHT **Sabretache of the 1st Croatian Hussar Regt, 1813, belonging to *Chef d'escadron* Pavlica. The initials 'IHC' (1er Hussards Croates) are picked out in silver below a silver crowned Imperial eagle on the plain black leather sabretache – see Plate G. (MIHT)**

Austrian *Hausmontur* uniforms faced yellow, with new locally-made brown trousers. The 1806 pattern shako is Austrian. The only French features are the red pompon and epaulettes of carabiniers, and the tricolour cockade.

G1: Sergeant, Croatian Hussar Regiment; Karlovac, 1813
This NCO wears campaign dress, which consisted of the iron-grey pelisse trimmed with black lambskin, worn over his sky-blue dolman with light buff facings, and overall trousers. The inside and cuffs of both the dolman and pelisse were reinforced with black leather, as are the overalls. His rank is displayed by two white chevrons on the lower sleeves. Above the shako cockade is a pompon in company colours; the plate cypher '1' is a reminder that at one time the raising of a second regiment was envisaged. Over his left shoulder he wears the doubled white leather crossbelt/sling for the cartridge pouch and carbine.

G2: Captain, Croatian Hussar Regiment; Italy, 1813
This officer wears his regulation full dress uniform, comprising a sky-blue dolman faced with 'buff' – in fact yellow – and trimmed with silver, an iron-grey pelisse and breeches. His rank is indicated by the red plume and the silver lace top band on his shako, and four silver chevrons on the cuffs of the dolman and pelisse. His breeches are also decorated with four silver laces, and lace on the side seams. His black cartridge box sling has silver mountings, while his sabre-tache is plain black leather with a silver imperial eagle over 'IHC'.

G3: Pioneer, Croatian Pioneers Battalion; Bourges, 1814
These former hussars sent to France retained many pieces of their previous uniforms, especially the shako and grey or green cavalry cloak/greatcoat *(manteau)* shown here. The pioneer is equipped with a sapper axe, which he carries in a black leather case on a white leather belt. Instead of boots he is wearing black shoes with black gaiters.

H1: Private, Albanian Regiment, 1808–14
The costume of these troops was of local origin, comprising a loose white 'Greek' shirt with a wide cloth waist sash, a sleeveless waistcoat often matching red or blue breeches, stockings or leggings, soft leather shoes, a cloak of coarse cloth used as a greatcoat or part of a tent, and either a red fez with a drooping black horsehair plume or a low cap with or without a turban on top. Note his shaven head and long scalplock. The armament comprised pistols, a 'Cretan' yataghan knife and a long flintlock gun.

H2: Officer, Albanian Regiment, 1808–14
The dress of officers and NCOs was of better quality and more richly ornamented; and note the archaic leg armour. Aside from a pair of pistols with the characteristic straight butts, armament often included a longer and more richly decorated yataghan, a sabre, or – as shown here – an antique Albanian sword.

H3: *Chasseur*, Septinsular Battalion, 1808–12
These chasseurs wore French light infantry uniform and equipment; the facings and piping were officially light blue, but faded to grey in the island sunshine. The battalion was allocated to the Italian Royal Army, so the shako cockade was red, white and green; a brass diamond-shaped shako plate was stamped 'BS' for 'Battaglione Septinsulaire'.

INDEX